Praise

MW01611261

"Brian Huskie is brilliantly angry--about what he experienced as a soldier in Iraq and has since experienced as a public school teacher in the US. The target of his anger is *compulsion.* Compulsion eliminates the possibility of real education in our schools and fails to improve the world in our international relationships. Regarding schools, Huskie has some useful advice for students who are stuck in them and for administrators and others who would like to remove the compulsion and return to students the possibility of self-respect, self-control, and meaningful learning."

~Peter Gray, Research Professor at Boston College and author of FREE TO LEARN: Why Releasing the Instinct to Play Will Make Our Children Happier, More Self-Reliant, and Better Students for Life.

"Moving and insightful, this book about teaching and learning is written by a military veteran who is now a public high school teacher. Brian Huskie's personal stories will grip you, and his thoughts about love, war, and school deserve our serious attention."

~Patrick Farenga, president of HoltGWS.com and publisher of Growing Without Schooling magazine.

"In A WHITE ROSE, Brian Huskie bares his soul as he grapples with what it means to be a veteran and a teacher, and with an educational system that doesn't always put students first. You'll find his story moving and inspirational."

~Daniel Pink, author of TO SELL IS HUMAN and DRIVE

Cheryl,
Thank You So much for Your
support!

[signature]

A WHITE ROSE:

A Soldier's Story of
Love, War, and School

BRIAN HUSKIE

OUTLAWED BOOKS

Outlawed Books
9 Lois Lane
Loudonville, NY 12211

www.BrianHuskie.com

ISBN: 0-9994137-0-8
ISBN-13: 978-0-9994137-0-8

Cover Design by Elisa Clare

1 3 5 7 9 10 8 6 4 2

First Edition

To Ramita, Rohan, and Navin.

For we walk by faith, not by sight.

CONTENTS

Part Two: A Letter to My Teenage Self

ACKNOWLEDGMENTS

Patrick Farenga, thank you for reading and commenting on an early version of this manuscript. Your words of encouragement came at precisely the right time.

Uncle Freddy (Alfred Cook), thank you for your significant financial backing, but even greater thanks for your much needed advice and support. It's not easy resurrecting ghosts.

Mario Garzia, thank you for your financial backing, both for this project and for your significant contribution to the Refugee Scholarship Endowment. You have been a good friend since we were five – a person doesn't get too many of those in a lifetime.

Carol Black, thank you for your financial backing of a relative stranger. I deeply respect your advocacy for peaceful education, and I am honored by your support.

Matt Russo, thank you for volunteering your time and expertise to edit this book line-by-line.

Rita and Rampada Paul, thank you for being the best mother- and father-in-law a person could ask for.

Olivia Parker, thank you for your help with the initial marketing of this book. Hold on to that enthusiasm!

Tethkar Ahmad, thank you for taking the time to interview me, for your thoughtful words, and for your continued friendship.

Also, thank you to all of my refugee students, who have shared so much of their story with me. There is no way my old brain could name you all without forgetting some. You know who you are, and you have had a profound effect on the very direction of my life.

Debbie and Dave Huskie, thank you for being my biggest fans.

Ramita, it takes a special kind of woman to live in a house with three crazy Huskie boys. You've dived in head-first, and for that, I could never repay you. What I can do is love you without limit.

1

PART ONE:
A RUTHLESS FORCE

Beat! Beat! Drums!

Beat! beat! drums!—blow! bugles! blow!
Through the windows—through doors—burst like a ruthless force,
Into the solemn church, and scatter the congregation,
Into the school where the scholar is studying,
Leave not the bridegroom quiet—no happiness must he have now
    with his bride,
Nor the peaceful farmer any peace, ploughing his field or gathering
    his grain,
So fierce you whirr and pound you drums—so shrill you bugles blow.

Beat! beat! drums!—blow! bugles! blow!
Over the traffic of cities—over the rumble of wheels in the streets;
Are beds prepared for sleepers at night in the houses? no sleepers
    must sleep in those beds,
No bargainers' bargains by day—no brokers or speculators—would
    they continue?
Would the talkers be talking? would the singer attempt to sing?
Would the lawyer rise in the court to state his case before the judge?
Then rattle quicker, heavier drums—you bugles wilder blow.

Beat! beat! drums!—blow! bugles! blow!
Make no parley—stop for no expostulation,
Mind not the timid—mind not the weeper or prayer,
Mind not the old man beseeching the young man,
Let not the child's voice be heard, nor the mother's entreaties,
Make even the trestles to shake the dead where they lie awaiting the
    hearses,
So strong you thump O terrible drums—so loud you bugles blow.

~Walt Whitman

1

A WHITE, WHITE ROSE

I was back in college within a week of returning from Iraq. I had begun my undergraduate odyssey in 1998 and it was 2005, so I was ready to be done. I was ready to finish a degree, start a career, get married, and have kids. I was twenty-five-years-old, and if all went as planned I figured by my thirties and forties I'd be able to spend my weekdays working and raising kids, and my weekends drinking beer with the vets at the VFW.

I'm that age now, but I've still never been inside a VFW, or even marched in a parade. It wasn't a conscious decision to avoid connecting with other veterans. I just didn't do it, with no real reason why. Or maybe Iraq was chasing me like an asteroid through space, and I didn't want to pause long enough for it to catch up. I didn't want to entertain the notion of PTSD or fear or alcohol addiction. I didn't want to hear about the suicides. I didn't want to swap war stories that seem so unreal in Albany, New York, that our truths sound like lies. I didn't want to face the possibility that the killing and destruction in Iraq had nothing to do with protecting freedom – that I had played a small but exuberant part in manufacturing war for profit.

I was all alone. I did get the degree, career, wife, and kids, but in the early years of all of that, I felt desperately alone. Nothing seemed particularly important. Even the news – *thirty killed in a car bomb in Baghdad* – was on a ticker under the main story of Brittany Spear's breakup or some other nonsense. *Jesus*, I thought. *Have any of these people seen thirty destroyed bodies, littering the marketplace, then stacked like firewood before being loaded onto a truck to be brought to the morgue in Tikrit?*

I still feel like an extraterrestrial if I try to talk about what "keeping America safe from terror" looks like in real life. Either I'm laughing at things that freak out the civilians, or I'm crying over things that were significantly less horrific than storming beaches in Normandy. I'd rather not feel like a baby or freak out the neighbors, but sometimes I drink too much just so I can summon the monster. Drag him out from under the bed and give him a little kiss. Then I wake up with a headache and pretend it didn't happen, and the little bastard goes back under the bed where he belongs.

Back in 2010, three or four years into public school teaching, the woman who taught the advanced English Language Learners retired. She recommended I take her job, she said, because I married an Indian woman and so that somehow made me the logical choice to teach foreigners. I formed a connection with several of the students, but one Iraqi girl in particular.

When I see her I see the boy, bullet scars and burns; I see the son flopping dead in his arms and kids in uniforms walking to school, and I remember how we used their desks for firewood. I see the Spiral Tower and the Golden Mosque. Samarra. Sulfur. I love you. I'm sorry. Now burn. She tells me how her uncle is lost in the Tigris. It will be her mother next if they don't leave soon. I have waking dreams: we blow up her house because that's where the men who extorted her father kept weapons. She waits for me after school with red inked English and math quizzes to cry over verb tense and mismarked decimals.

She tells me about a song they used to sing about a white, white rose, and writes it on my chalkboard in Arabic. When the students go home and I sit in the classroom, pretending to grade papers, I look at the song and I start to cry. It's in Arabic and I don't know the words. It's a white rose and I don't know how I got on this road and I want off but I keep going, because I need a job but also because I was born with a permanent screw you *attitude, and there's no way I could ever walk away from this much pain. It's a swamp with beautiful white roses everywhere. You can just see them through the fog and ghosts.*

I was with one other soldier at a traffic control point when two Iraqi kids came over to talk to us. They wanted to go buy kabobs for us and charge us triple for them. They also wanted our 5.56mm rounds so they could scrape the bullet off and light the gun powder. We teased them for a few minutes, haggling over kabobs and lighting matches. The older one tried to get us to give him a grenade for a couple of kabobs. The soldier who was with me pretended to throw the grenade. He didn't even have it in his hand – it was in good fun – but the younger one stumble-ran into the weeds and started crying. He was bawling. He wouldn't let anyone near him. I took off my helmet and gave up my gun and brought the kid a Gatorade. He whirled around and hugged me, and as we hugged in the weeds time lost meaning. When I hug my four year old I sometimes feel that little Iraqi boy's ribs. He showed me the scars on his leg. He had been burned from his ankle to his thigh. He was covered in scars. He made a machine gun noise, pointed to his leg, and said *Amerikee!*

For the fourth of July, 2014, ten years after Iraq, I went with my family to Montauk beach to watch the fireworks and my youngest, two-years-old, was terrified. He tried to run away high up on a sand dune. I ran after him, caught him, picked him up and tried to console him. The kid just went limp. My son didn't move, didn't make a sound, and just fell asleep, almost instantly. I'm kicking in doors and raiding homes. There's a man, he has some kind of certificate signed by Saddam Hussein and he doesn't look scared. His son, less than five, in the upstairs room. There is shooting and yelling, and the kid just sleeps. I pick him up and brought him to his mother, and although he was unhurt he wouldn't wake up. My son just goes limp in my arms.

We took over a hospital and, after a day of fighting, a man brought his son in. The son was obviously dead...maybe seven or eight-years-old. He was flopping around in his dad's arms. The father was laughing uncontrollably – maniacally. I'll never forget it. *It happens, says an Iraqi student, many years later. A man was killed a week before his wedding. His mother was laughing, too. She said it will be alright, she said her son is still alive. His fiancé runs home and changes into her wedding dress. His body is in the house, and they both danced around it, laughing, saying he was alive, that he wasn't dead. Nobody could stop them. The mother didn't have any other family. She was dead within the month. The fiancé was sent away to the place where they send all the crazy people.*

When I see my students I see the crowds of little kids who begged for pencils and candy; I see the kids who walked to school until they canceled school so we could fight. I break their desks to burn to keep warm in December, and our sniper takes a position in an elementary classroom. I see the boy whose leg was burned, and the little limp sleeper who had guns pointed at him, and the laughing dad. I see them in my own kids. It haunts me.

These kids from Iraq, as well as refugees from other places in the Middle East, Africa, Burma, and Nepal, didn't choose to have war or persecution happen to them. They didn't choose the actions of their countries or of ours. They all have their own stories, but somehow, they made it here. They have an obligation to make the most out of their lives, and they know it. It's a second chance many don't get. What are they going to do with this new life they were given?

I was given a second chance, too. When I first got back from Iraq I was angry. I wanted to fight "9/11 Truthers," anyone critical of President Bush (who had blessed us all with the opportunity to go kill bad guys and prove ourselves), anyone critical of the war or invasion, anyone who suggested that terror isn't real or that American soldiers aren't the good guys or that they sometimes do bad things. My family has a dozen combat veterans; I saw the rubble from the twin towers; I put my life on the line, I was shot at, blown up, and crashed-up. Have you ever put your life, and the life of everyone around you, both friend and foe, on the line for a belief? Not your career. Not your GPA. Your actual, literal, life. I have. I dare you to challenge that belief.

That's how I felt, and so I know how people feel when I say things like "teachers aren't the most important factor in the learning process" and "school resembles prison" and "compulsion is violence." I get it, just as I didn't want to look Iraq in the eye and say *maybe killing people and breaking their stuff isn't the best way to spread love, peace, freedom, and democracy*, no teacher wants to look their students in the eye and say *maybe bribing and threatening you and your parents isn't the best way to offer education that's effective, respectful, and caring.* Teachers do care, and they do want to help students. However, one definition of culture is "the way we do things around here" and our culture says to separate your children from yourself...and your dangerous traditions...and your medieval religions...and your attitudes towards sex...and your attitudes towards money...and your other perverted ideals...and have strangers raise them from ages five to eighteen. Then structure everything to incentivize these young adults to indebt themselves financially to institutions of higher learning. This indentured servitude will last for the majority of their adult life, during which time they will have fleeting moments of wondering who they are and where they fit into society, but most of the time they'll distract themselves with touchscreens.

One of the most common questions students will ask me, when they find out I was in Iraq, is, *are you any different? Are you crazy now?* I was a little crazy before I signed up, truth be told, but I am different now, though it took a while to sort out exactly how. I learned something they can't teach in school, something institutions around the globe rather you not learn.

I came to terms with my mortality. Like in the poem *The Twa Corbies*, when I die, nobody is going to know where I went, my dog and hawk and lady will move on with their lives, and naught but the wind will blow over my bones for evermore.

Figuratively, of course. I assume somebody will mourn me. With luck I die somewhere near people, so they'll know where my corpse is, and they'll do something with that corpse and so they'll know where that is, too. (The week before we went to Iraq, the Chaplain said to us, *I want to die like my grandfather; peacefully in his sleep. I don't want to die screaming and on fire, like the passengers in my grandfather's car*). Yet the memories of us are finite. In three or four generations there will be no one alive who ever met you. Given enough time you'll leave no trace of your existence, in print or memory. It's not just our bodies that return to the ether.

Most people I know are either scared of dying and so they avoid thinking and talking about it, or they don't care and so they have no reason to think about it or talk about it. The ones who don't care shrug it off as something mechanical, something biological and unavoidable except by pretending it doesn't exist, and wave it off as a nuisance thing that may catch up with you someday, but doesn't matter now. What matters now is personally consuming whatever can be accumulated.

Denying your mortality out of fear or indifference is denying your humanity. When you deny your humanity then you deny the humanity of others, and the sanctity of all life on the planet. Machines don't care if they hurt feelings, destroy the environment, skip out on responsibilities, or play on their smart phone all day. When I see students who are physically unable to put their phones away, I can't help but to picture a tree that's wrapped itself around a telephone pole. At some point their hands will grow skin around those damned things, and they'll have to plug themselves in at night.

It's not enough to act fearless towards death. You have to acknowledge the deadline. Iraq made me do that. I saw lots of dead people. I'm not saying it doesn't bother me to think about, or that I'm personally in a rush to die. What I am saying is that if you don't accept death as inevitable, then it's much easier to allow yourself to be controlled by the irrelevant. When you come to terms with being finite, you prioritize. If your doctor told you that you have six weeks to live, then I bet you'd spend less time liking-and-sharing memes and more time telling grandma you love her. As your unofficial medical counsel, I need to tell you that you have only some number of weeks left. The moment you were born you jumped out of the airplane, and the only thing you don't know was how high the plane was.

There are humans and there are machines. Institutions would prefer machines over humans because machines are programmable, predictable, and replaceable. It's why we teach sex education and not philosophy in school. Better to learn about the plumbing than explore what it means to be human. *But students need sex education because there is a danger in them not knowing about AIDS and condoms.* There is a greater danger in students not having the opportunity to come to terms with their mortality and the implication that has on their life, or the liberty in realizing that all you are is borrowed, and all the world is a playground.

Humans are turned into machines when our work owns us and not us our work. African slaves were machines designed to work the fields; they weren't given the right of humanity, namely, personal sovereignty, community, culture, and family. "Property," while accurate, isn't a specific enough term. They were machines. Given enough time of having a master, and having that master demand tasks of you, you will lose your humanity. There were at least some freed slaves who lamented the end of slavery.[1] Goldfish only know the water

---

[1] "Some narratives contain startling descriptions of cruelty while others convey a nostalgic view of plantation life."
http://www.loc.gov/teachers/classroommaterials/connections/narratives-slavery/file.html

that's in their bowl.

Factory workers on a furniture assembly line are less satisfied with themselves as people than are custom furniture builders, regardless of pay and benefits. On the assembly line, the master assigns the task and the machine performs. The worker is subservient to the apparatus. If you are assigned work, and have no option to quit that work without being penalized, you are being co-opted by machinery. You are being prepped for college and career, that is, you are moving down the conveyor belt, assembled by other robots who were assembled long ago in a similar factory who are all being held accountable by an even bigger and colder machine. You are being taught that you have an input and an output and someone can push a button to make you dance. Given enough time, leaving that situation can be painful, but even if the physical conditions of your enslavement are good, giving up your personal sovereignty is never good for your humanity.

In school, nobody ever asked me, *Do you think about dying? Where do you think you go when you die? How do you feel about your mortality?* To my knowledge, no teacher would ever ask a student that in the district I work, or any other district. It's not in the curriculum. It took a year in a war zone for me to confront one of the most awesome and overwhelming abilities we have, something no other being on earth can do: the capacity to consider our personal death and what that means for our life. You don't know what you're giving up if you ignore that in your humanity.

I don't separate "education" – a special thing done in a special place by specialized, certified people, during a special period in a person's life – and life itself. My experience in Iraq in 2004 has made me afraid for my oldest son, who feels as deeply as I do, and who has as hard a time forgetting the capitals of states as I do the bright white flash and return-fire.

Four years into teaching I had a Dominican girl in class who was terrified of public speaking, even in front of our class of ten. I more or less forced her, using every coercive teacher trick I knew, because I was always taught to face your fears. I'm not sure if that was the right thing to do. She was trembling even after she was finished, and although she kept coming to class, she cowered in the last-seat-last-row for the rest of the year. She volunteered for nothing more. I wrote about my experience in Iraq because I've always been told to "just talk about it, you'll feel better." Unless you're ready, that advice is shit.

What is education but life itself? Like Tim O'Brien alluded to in *The Things They Carried*, there is no moral. He writes, "in the end, really, there's nothing much to say about a true war story, except maybe 'Oh.'" I'd probably use a different word than "oh." Lessons?

We smashed their schools, burned them, and shot people based on the time of night they were outside. They dressed up like our allies and blew themselves up, when they weren't murdering the families of our actual allies and throwing their headless bodies into the Tigris. Write a five paragraph essay on that. Or write about how we've lost more soldiers to suicide than to combat. Your choice. Make sure each paragraph has a topic sentence.

Being lawful and following the rules means allowing their reality to become your reality, and their reality includes you pledging your allegiance to their republic before you're old enough know what the words "allegiance" or "republic" mean. School is a photocopy of life. It's a combination of *Office Space* and the eye of Sauron. It primes you for reliance on others. It has the illusion of a beginning, middle, and end, and the illusion of progress, but then you wake up and realize there is no moral. Education, if such a thing even exists. I just call it life. There are tears, laughter, regret, love, and patience. There's empathy and apathy. There's living and dying. If you're going to give a single person a single grade for that, you might as well fail me. I'm not playing and I'm done running from Iraq.

2

LOVE, WAR, AND SCHOOL

A rocket propelled grenade (RPG) slammed into the concrete bunker. I had been sitting outside of it – the bunker was lined with sandbags. A bright white dirty flash and I was deaf from the explosion, laying on my back, enveloped in a cloud of dirt and dust. I jumped to my feet, disoriented. Like the movie *The Matrix*, bullets came through the cloud in slow motion, and they seemed to streak by every single place except where I was. I saw the machine gunner on the ground in the bunker, writhing, and my first thought was his guts had been blown out, but later I discovered he was (like me) unscathed. The other guy with us was also rolling on the ground – we found out later his eardrum was destroyed. Someone switched reality from slow motion to fast forward, and I ran around the bunker to where my weapon had landed. I unleashed every high explosive grenade I had, hitting buildings and vehicles. The guy in the bunker reached up and grabbed his machine gun with one hand and let loose. The guys on the roof to the left, and my buddy to the right, who had been inside, also joined the symphony of automatic weapons.

When it was done, it was done. Someone had poked out of an alley and fired an RPG, and I guess a couple more guys fired at us with rifles without really aiming. We returned fire, the Iraqi Police who were with us hid, and that was about it. This was three weeks before our tour was over. We helped train the next group of soldiers, and I paired up with someone named Staff Sergeant Olson for a patrol. The patrol went without incident, but Sergeant Olson was killed two weeks later when he walked in front of an improvised explosive device. *Was the haji who set the IED the same motherfucker who almost killed me with an RPG? Or had I mortally wounded him with a grenade?* I told myself I had, but I doubt it.

In the days that followed the RPG attack I noticed a change. I couldn't read. When I picked up a magazine or a book, all of the words and letters would scrunch together and blur, and when I tried to focus, I couldn't. I would stare, virtually unblinking, for hours down the road where the attack came from, my weapon's safety off, my finger on the trigger. *This guy tried to kill me, he's out there, and I'm going to blow his fucking head off.* Nothing happened for a few weeks, then we went to Kuwait, then we went home to New York, and I was in a bunch of undergraduate English classes within thirty days of landing at Fort Drum. Although my ability to focus had improved, I still struggled to get through a chapter without my vision clouding and my heart racing.

Much earlier in our tour I accompanied Special Forces; I'm not certain, but I think it was to a suburb of Balad. It was an especially dangerous mission because of the possibility of friendly fire. There were several units involved, and the Iraqi Central Defense Corps (ICDC) had been left in the dark, since it was known that more than half of them worked for both sides. I manned the machine gun on the Humvee. It's tough to be brave when Special Forces soldiers look scared before a mission. ICDC lived in the apartment complex we were raiding, and it was likely going to be a shit-show trying to shoot the right people while not getting shot by the wrong people.

We drive into the building complex with the lights off, using night vision goggles, but Humvees aren't very quiet, so we go to white lights pretty quickly. The Special Forces team raids a building and the rest of us keep the perimeter secure. They kill someone in the apartment and pull out quickly. Someone is shooting at us, but I have no idea where it is coming from. The team loads back into the truck and we whip around the way we came.

Back at the part of the complex where we had entered, there were huge holes in a building that weren't there before. An ICDC lay dead, some blood smeared on his face, though besides that, and the fact he was dead, he didn't look too bad. Another ICDC, living, was on his knees next to a pile of burnt garbage, and he let out a wail like I had never heard. He howled, then leveled his eyes to mine. He was in pain. My eyes adjusted to the pile of melted garbage by his knees and it was then that I could make out the head and torso. "It's his brother," the driver said to me, and the man on his knees kept staring at me. A bunch of ICDC had rushed out of the building, brandishing their weapons and firing randomly. The Bradley Fighting Vehicle, still parked about 300 yards away, took them out. The surviving ICDC wanted answers. The Special Forces Captain surveyed the situation, looked at the interpreter, and said, "Tell them it was an RPG."

This "war," if you want to call it that, was known as "Operation Iraqi Freedom" and ended, sort of, in 2011. As of this writing, ISIS, a force more powerful, better funded, better trained, and more brutal than either the Taliban or Al Qaeda, occupy Iraq, and continue to rape children, murder homosexuals or non-Sunni Muslims, sell women into bondage, and have attempted genocide on the Yazidi people. The Taliban beheaded little girls for the crime of learning how to read, and their leadership declared ISIS to be too extreme. In contrast, the United States has the technologically most advanced, funded, trained, and lethal military that has ever existed in the history of killing one another. You would think that after fifteen years of war on terror, waged by a country with nuclear submarines, all terror on earth would be destroyed. I'm shocked that nary a nightmare has made it out alive. Yet somehow, killing the shit out of people – thousands and thousands of people – doesn't make the living not scared. What you do wind up with are millions of refugees and armies of genocidal fanatics.

Love is freedom; hate and fear is slavery. When we live in a state of *internalized* love, we become a cloud or a wave; *Have you ever seen a cloud that is misshaped? Have you ever seen a badly designed wave?*[2] We become more in sync with the universe, and while we will always at times feel anger, jealousy, and shame, and we will always make mistakes in the material world, if we live in love then we have the foundation to be able to grow internally as a result of whatever happens outside our heart. When you choose to love, you will love no matter what people do to you, your relationship to them, or whether or not you even know them. You will love villagers in China who haven't even been born yet! How? Because your love for mankind has, or should have, nothing to do with the *external.* You love your spouse because of what is inside you; your love begins and ends in your being. She doesn't feed you love; she can't stop feeding you and cause you to hate. You have the ability to choose love. Whether I love or hate the man who tried to kill me, that's energy that is happening in my heart. It has nothing to do with anything else.

We best live and learn having cultivated an internalized sense of love. In schools, we reward and punish. We grade and rank. We emphasize job-training such as *college and career readiness* and use data to inform instruction. The well-known Bible verse reads *for the love of money is the root of all evil* (1Timothy6:10). It's not that *money is the root of all evil.* That's absurd. *The love of money is the root of all evil.* When we cultivate an internal state of love, we exude peace. When our

---

[2] Alan Watts

love is for currency, or any of the things that currency brings, we are flirting with something dangerous. What are grades but a kind of fiat currency? How many students would do a teacher's work if it didn't count as a grade? How many would compromise their principles for a grade? What grades do is turn "learning" into a task you complete in return for a reward, which instills a dependency on external stimuli. It robs opportunity for an internalized sense of love for what the student is doing. It makes the student want to throw their books over a cliff as soon as the assigned task is completed (more on throwing books over a cliff later).

Choice is implicit in peace and love. Homework is your responsibility the same way it was the slaves' responsibility to pick cotton. What else do you call it when a stranger makes you do work you didn't agree to in order to benefit a system into which you're compelled by law to participate? You behave differently when you are engaged in an activity you love and where there are actual consequences. In this way, caring for a pet hamster for a month offers more opportunity for personal growth than an entire year of "required classes" that a combination of state and school district strangers decided was your responsibility.

Your mind and heart are the only things that can't be imprisoned by other people unless you allow them to be. If you allow yourself to be manipulated by people or things, and you love them for what they say or what they give you, then you become a slave to them. The same goes for choice; you don't grow without having choice in your intellectual and emotional responsibilities.

The opposite of independence is dependence. So long as we have our minds, freedom can never be taken from us; we can however relinquish freedom, usually bit by bit without ever realizing. Here's the real danger…when you allow others to plan your life long enough, you grow accustomed to it and you become dependent. You allow yourself to be subservient to the machine, and not the other way around. You need to be able to make mindful conscious decisions or else you're simply plodding blindly along towards someone else's goal. You cannot bring peace through violence. You cannot bring love through fear and hate. You cannot have freedom in a state of coercion marked by bribes and threats. This goes as much for war as it does for school. We will never win the war on terror with war. We will never have a peaceful, loving society, so long as most kids go through schools that utterly disrespect what makes them human.

I'll pause to warn the reader. Independent thinkers are the enemies of the state and her incestual lover commercialism, neither of whom exist without your choice to be dependent on them. There are dangers to taking books like this seriously.

3

CONSENT IS SEXY

I had a senior who came running into my class, showing off a button that read *Consent is Sexy* and very interested in "honest but uncomfortable conversations" with peers. If I remember, the *Gay-Straight Alliance*, in collaboration with school staff, had a bunch of these things made and were handing them out at lunch. Apparently the indomitable wave of college campus rapes is the result of a conspicuous lack of gay kids with pins.

But sure. I agree. Consent is "sexy." I'm just shocked that the irony is lost. First of all, my wife and I homeschool our kids, and usually the first "tough" question friends and family ask is *what about socialization*, i.e., how will they learn how to interact with peers? Well, here we are, at public school where all the wonderful socialization happens, and we find it necessary to remind seventeen- and eighteen-year-olds, in writing, not to have sex with people who don't agree to have sex. Whatever "socialization" means, it should include the knowledge and ability to not rape (preferably without reminders).

Second of all, *Consent is Sexy* pins were handed out in *compulsory* school where students don't have the opportunity to consent to anything. They have virtually no say in which classes they take, they certainly have no say in what is taught or how it is taught once they get in those classes, they don't get to use the bathroom without written permission, homework isn't a mutually agreed upon voluntary activity; students eat when they're told to eat, move when they're told to move, speak when they're told to speak, write when they're told to write, and so on. They are never once asked by anyone for permission to have these things done to them. *Compulsion* means to be forced to do something; *consent* means agreeing to do something. There is nothing consensual about school. No wonder we need buttons.

Compulsory education is an ineffective way to teach and learn, as well as antithetical to the principles of freedom upon which this country was founded. Yes, I know that much of those past freedoms were freedoms for white Protestant males. I'm not denying that, but that important fact also isn't a sufficient reason to deny freedoms to more groups in the future. In fact, the "scientific" reasons given for denying groups rights in the past are similar to the reasons given to deny teenagers rights now: slaves should not be given freedom because they would not be able to handle it – blacks by their nature are lazy and violent and therefore must be controlled; women should not be allowed to vote because they are ignorant and a woman's brain can only handle so much complex thought before they become ugly and infertile; teenagers should not direct their own learning because if not pushed to do something then they would choose to do nothing (lazy), with the exception of drugs, sex, video games, and fighting (ignorant, violent, and must be controlled).

There are a few assumptions that I'm going to make about teenagers and education:

- A teenager's nature is not laziness, their preferred state is not ignorance, and it is not necessary for extrinsic motivation to be delivered by trained professionals in order to prevent them from bareknuckle boxing under a bridge in exchange for drugs and money.

- Teenagers aren't broken, and so we don't need to fix them.

- Just because a student complies doesn't mean they are engaged; just because they can recite data doesn't mean they've gained knowledge or wisdom.

- A teenager is not a child. They are ready for real responsibility. Suggesting that they, for example, should be required to obtain written permission to use the bathroom is a humiliating affront to their dignity. The same goes with force-feeding Shakespeare and algebra.

- An underdeveloped prefrontal cortex, i.e. the reason why teenagers are impulsive, is as much a gift as it is a curse, and is not a reason to lock teenagers up in a series of rooms all day. Either God or Darwin or both made us that way for a reason. Risk-taking is good. Danger is good. Adventure is good. You don't get to be old and wise unless you are young and dumb. Cutting teens off from adventure produces adults who are timid and neurotic.

- "Education" is not something that only happens in certain places at certain times with certain well-trained people. School is optional. Independent thought and action is your birthright, no matter what anyone tries to fill your head with.

- Teachers are not the enemy – they are, for the most part, loving, patient, competent people with a drive to help students achieve. The enemies are not students, school administrators, parents, or school boards. Even politicians aren't the bad guys in our story (they aren't the good guys, either). The insidious notion that permeates most of our society – that teenagers won't learn unless we force them, and the ones who are best equipped to force them are school-people – this *idea* is the enemy. Nothing will change politically until we as a society call out this myth for what it is.

Even if you resist the notion that *schools are prisons* or that *teenagers aren't inherently lazy or dangerous*, if we could come to agreement on some of these points, then we have some common ground upon which to start our journey.

"I need your help figuring out what these questions are asking," a fellow teacher asked me. She had fourteen multiple choice questions from the New York common core Regents exam, which is required for graduation. Next to the questions she had another paper with four main categories – analyze, inference, etc. – and a bunch of subcategories underneath. We dutifully read the poem and the multiple choice questions and began the process of categorizing, so we could later collect data from students' answers and quietly use the outputs to inform our inputs.

"This is stupid," I said, but continued working.

"I know," she said half-heartedly. We have known each other for a decade. I think we both knew I was about to rant, and one of us didn't really want to hear it. *When you work at the burger joint, and the boss tells you to salt the fries, you salt the fries,* I imagined she was thinking. *No need to turn fry-salting into a bid for congress.*

"What if the poet himself doesn't know what he is inferring?" I circled *author's purpose* for number seven. "What if he doesn't know his own purpose? What if this is just some deep expression of something he's feeling but can't otherwise articulate? Or what if he *thinks* he knows his purpose for writing, but every single reader takes it differently? What if he is expressing something about his life or his experience that he can never properly understand himself? What if he doesn't get his own motivations?"

She put down her pencil and smiled politely. "I think

you're overthinking it. Just, on its face, your first instinct – what's the question asking? We need to know which performance indicator to teach."

We finished, the work day finished, and I left the school building. On the way home I stopped by the grocery store to pick up something for dinner, and while waiting in line I mindlessly scrolled through my social media. At the top of my timeline was a link shared by a group I follow: *I Can't Answer These Texas Standardized Test Questions About My Own Poems.*[3] Sara Holbrook writes:

> *Did I have a purpose for writing it? Does survival count? Teachers are also trying to survive as they are tasked with teaching kids how to take these tests, which they do by digging through past tests, posted online. Forget joy of language and the fun of discovery in poetry, this is line-by-line dissection, painful and delivered without anesthetic.*

The universe speaks to us in coincidence. We can hear it if we listen. When we don't pay attention, or when we hear but don't heed, then we set ourselves up for failure. The energy of the universe flows around you, and choosing to swim against the current will lead to nothing but exhaustion.

This is why our education system fails to educate. Learning is social and playful. Mammals wrestle and play tag in order to do all the things necessary for survival. They do not take seriously the training they are doing for the most serious parts of their lives – catching prey, eluding predators, establishing enough dominance to secure a mate, and raising young. It is meant to be joyful.

How many times have I told students that, when answering essay questions on a test, *it doesn't matter what you think, it matters what you can* support *using the textual evidence in front of you. You're not trying to change the world, you're trying to pass*

---

[3] http://www.huffingtonpost.com/entry/standardized-tests-are-so-bad-i-cant-answer-these_us_586d5517e4b0c3539e80c341

23

a test. Literature is meant to be playful – but so is physics. If you aren't on the playground, it's going to show in whatever you create. You will produce one lifeless piece of cardboard after another before they finally print you a degree, which itself probably won't even be on cardboard.

Compulsion – nonconsensual education – requires violence; it requires complete control over what students put into their brain, the people they are exposed to, the places they are authorized to be, and oftentimes, with free lunch programs, what food goes into their body. Compulsory systems are resentful of families who do not enforce homework or dress code policies; are reluctant to allow parents into its buildings except once or twice a year on special "open house" days; and fear parents who choose to homeschool. It is damn near the most unnatural way a human of any age can authentically learn. Can you imagine a couple of puppies being forced to wrestle under threat of in-school suspension, while a well-trained expert looks on with a clipboard, marking off points?

I'm not interested in "reforming" education. I don't care about tinkering with the curriculum or bickering over charters and vouchers. I'm interested in revolting against compulsion. Cotton fields and tobacco farms are amoral things. You can be an abolitionist and still see the value in T-shirts and cob pipes. If you're an abolitionist, then what you are against is slavery, and what you are for is freedom – freedom for individuals to live their lives any way they choose, so long as what they choose doesn't infringe on others to do the same. I'm not calling for the end of public schools. I'm calling for the end of compulsion.

Compulsory education is against the law of nature. There are a number of people who are very upset about the possibility of transgender bathrooms in public schools, and they'll cite the same reason. If you're uncomfortable with the idea of transgender bathrooms because it goes against the natural order of things, but you see nothing unnatural with using the force of law to separate a child from their family and culture from the ages of five to seventeen, to be fed and taught by strangers during the best part of their waking hours, then I'm sorry, but we're probably not going to have much in common.

The grading policy is the whip that keeps the whole thing moving. Here's your homework assignment. Ask a dozen teachers, *what is the purpose behind grading students?* I don't know for sure what they'll tell you, but whatever they say will likely fall into one of three categories: Teachers prone to euphemism will say *to check for student understanding.* A well-intentioned teacher who spends considerable thought to assessment may say *to give feedback to the students and their parents.* The authoritarians prefer *to hold students (teachers, parents, etc.) accountable* – these are the same people who will say *they'll have a boss one day, won't they?* (nothing screams *cultivating a love of learning* louder than *your boss is here to hold you accountable*).

The first two categories you could do without an alpha-numeric score. I could tell a student what grade I thought they would receive on an essay based on a rubric and exemplars (but I'd rather not – after all, I'm not writing this book based on a rubric), or the writings overall effectiveness based on peer or public review, or ask them good questions after an oral presentation, or report to their parents how many hours they spent at their internship. Nothing done in typical *or* radical schools requires a recorded grade on a transcript in order to check student understanding or communicate with parents, and definitely not down to a single percentage point (somebody please tell me the difference between an 86% and an 87%). Furthermore, if grades were an objective and accurate reflection of a student's knowledge and skill, then why do we have "honors" ceremonies and give kids special diplomas, stickers, pizza, bagels, juice, and other little treats for performing as we wish them to? This isn't a competition they signed up for. It's something they are forced into, they are stripped bare to expose their strengths and weaknesses, then they are told they are good and given a treat as if they were a dog that learned to sit.

Ask a teacher of a non-credit bearing course what their greatest struggle is. Those are the teachers who beg and plead for teeth to their programs; they need some way to grade for accountability purposes. They'll tell you their daily struggle is attendance and student buy-in. Therein lays your answer. The purpose in grading students is coercion. It works equally as a bribe as it does a threat, with the unfortunate (unintended? I doubt it) consequence of training students to anticipate a stranger's valuation of an arbitrary and narrow curriculum as a superior indication of worth than intrinsic valuation of a self-directed, limitless curriculum. The result is a system that conditions students for boredom. Nothing worth doing could possibly be boring.

The *but you'll have a boss one day* people are actually tipping their hand as to what school is really all about. Governments require that the people be dependent on them in order for the government to remain viable – the more independent we are, the less relevant they become. Therefore, government schools would do well to get kids used to having a stranger as the arbitrary authority figure that is necessary in their lives. We could drop the pretense of school and just put students into jobs, if we're worried about their ability to listen to a boss, although the reality is it doesn't take twelve years of school to figure out what a boss does. That still doesn't properly address the dangers in treating absolute compliance to a series of strangers as a principle worth living by.

Growing up I loved John Updike's story "A&P" about a boy who quits his job after the store manager embarrasses three teenage girls in bikinis. When I was in my early twenties I had a retail job, and my boss had me follow a young black man about my same age around the store. I had followed suspicious people before, black and white, but this time seemed different, and by the end of it I realized I had been a participant in unfairly racially profiling someone. I wasn't as cool as Sammy from "A&P" – I didn't walk out and quit on the spot – but I started looking for a new job right away, and pretty soon after that I gave my two-weeks' notice. A boss isn't the same as a leader, a leader doesn't need state-sponsored compulsion or grades for people to follow them, and compliance is a value best reserved for dogs.

Grading learning is sacrilegious, and will inevitably lead to a corruption of learning. It is not learning at all, but a training in dependence and subservience. We are learning creatures; it's in our DNA. We aren't as strong as bears or as sturdy as goats, but we can build a house to live in, a gun to shoot the bear, and a stove to cook him up with a bit of butter from the goat. Nothing else on earth can do that, and it happens through an automatic drive for knowledge. We could wave a wand and make all schools in the world disappear, and learning will still keep on keeping on much as it has for the past ten thousand years. It's natural and healthy because it is in our instinct to survive.

Our eating habits are distinctly human, too. We sit down with the people we like or love, often give thanks and go through little rituals like pass dishes around to every member or remain seated until everyone is finished. We rarely eat with people we dislike, or with strangers, unless absolutely necessary. We eat like that for the same reason we love, empathize, and, synonymous with learn, play. It's gratifying for us. It strengthens us as individuals, families, and communities. It teaches us about ourselves and those around us. It makes us physically healthy.

The graded versions of these things are hotdog-eating contests, spelling bees, matchmaking reality shows, recitals, trivia games, standardized tests, and so on. They are quantifiable because they are specific; you can peg it with a percentage or rate contestants hierarchically. Genuine learning can never be quantified. None of the quantifiable stuff is the natural way of learning things except for when it is done just for fun. If taken too seriously, or for too long, or under threat, none of it is healthy.

Benjamin Franklin said *He's the best physician that knows the worthlessness of most medicines.* The "medical model" is often used as an analogy for education:[4] your graduation rate is your "survival" rate, thus your students who fail to graduate in four years is your "mortality" rate, and any choice by the school to emphasize social-emotional over data-driven-standards-aligned is akin to a doctor saying, "I didn't take your blood pressure, but I *feel* as though you're just fine." It's the worst metaphor I've ever heard for what learning is; not only for the fear necessary for making such an argument work (you're killing kids by not using data!), but for the insidious assumption that kids are "sick" and that we school-people are the only ones with the cure. It's the way we rationalize the compulsion and ensuing violence: if we don't make them, they won't, and it'll be chaos in the streets. I'm leery of any fear-based argument.

The natural state of kids isn't "sickness;" or, to put another way, ignorant, lazy, violent, unmotivated, indifferent, evil, etc. As controversial as this statement may be, kids are not going to revert to savages or drooling vegetables if they don't get *n* credits by *x*th grade.

I'm not against schools if treated as learning centers, but their purpose isn't to fix kids. Fix them? I didn't know they were broken! School vision statements often read something like, "We believe all kids can learn" or "life-long learners" or something silly like that. What an absurd thing to put in writing! "We, at Grassy Hill Elementary, believe all Kindergarteners can get taller" or "We, the Prospect Junior High cafeteria staff, believe that all kids can and will eat food." A human being's natural state is curiosity. I've described myself as an advocate of self-directed education, but truth be told, all learning comes from the self, so in a sense, "self-directed education" is redundant. Students will be life-long learners, of one thing or another; they will deliberately pursue their own dreams, or unconsciously pursue someone else's. Either way they are learning self-

---

[4] 'Do No Harm'. A Hippocratic Oath for Schools
http://www.edweek.org/ew/articles/2014/09/05/03stewart.h34.html

sufficiency, or else they are learning compliance.

Data has become my least favorite four letter word. Felix Baumgartner used data to inform some of his decisions when he jumped out of a frickin' space pod and plunged the 120,000 feet back to earth, but something tells me the data wasn't the central thing in his heart and mind throughout the entire process. Neither was what "grade" he was going to get – it was a pass/fail proposition. Data was the central concern of trainers and technicians, not the driving force for the man on the mission to be the first space-jumper in human history. I don't see great teachers as trainers or technicians. I'm sure if Socrates were alive today, and had to sit through even a single meeting discussing how to use data to inform instruction, he'd kill himself all over again.

Benjamin Franklin also said that any fool can complain, and most fools do, so I'll offer a better metaphor. John Taylor Gatto spoke of education being a "helix sport:"

Here's a principle of real education to carry you through the moments of self-doubt. Education is a helix sport, a unique personal project like seatless unicycle riding over trackless wilderness, a sport that avoids rails, rules, and programmed confinement. The familiar versions of this are cross-country skiing, sailing, hang-gliding, skateboarding, surfing, solitary mountain climbing, thousand-mile walks, things like that. I think of education as one, too.

In a helix sport the players search for a new relationship with themselves. They endure pain and risk to achieve this goal. Helix sports are free of expert micromanagement. Experts can't help you much in that moment of truth when a mistake might leave you dead. Helix sports are a revolt against predestination. Bringing children up properly is a helix sport forcing you to realize that no boy or girl on earth is just like another. If you do understand this you also understand there can exist no reliable map to tell you all you need to do. Process kids like sardines and don't be surprised when they come out oily and dead. In the words of the Albany Free School, if you aren't

29

making it up as you go along, you aren't doing it right.

4

EDUCATING THE NEXT GENERATION

I have no idea how I got this job as a teacher. My main focus when I was actually in high school was football, lunch, and making hell for my bus drivers. I failed out of college, but leveraged the *I went to Iraq and learned valuable lessons about responsibility and commitment and studying and the importance of education and flossing twice a day and on and on* to trick the University into accepting me into a teaching program. I interviewed for a job directly after certification.

I bombed my interview. You might think, *everyone says they bomb their interview. I'm sure it couldn't have been that bad.* It has been over a decade, and there are people who were on the interview panel whom I still have trouble looking in the eye. I'm embarrassed to think about it. I had a fancy leather folder with a silly little notepad inside, and I was trembling so violently that I couldn't read my notes afterwards. They asked something simple like *why do you want to teach here?* There was a full minute of complete silence before I gave a six second answer, and my supervisor, who I student-taught under (and who really wanted to hire me), had to nudge me and ask me if I'd like to add anything to that answer. I made a joke that nobody laughed at, and so I did the only logical thing and laughed by myself. They asked which books I had most recently read, and my best answer was *Retiling Bathrooms for Dummies*. At some point I think I used the word "Nazis," although I can't remember the context. It was bad. They hired me, and I don't know why, but I promise you, dear reader, the interview was pathetic.

I'm not generally a nervous person. I didn't expect to be nervous during the interview. What happened? For one, I was in the principal's office. The last time I was sitting in front of a principal, bullshitting answers, I was fifteen-years-old and had just been caught climbing on the back of the basketball hoop. All of my experiences suggest that there is no good reason to be sitting in front of a school principal. The second reason I already alluded to in the keyword *bullshitting*. I was aware that I was a fraud, and self-conscious of the "fact" that no one else was. It was my assumption that skilled teachers spent their days imparting important and meaningful knowledge to eager students. I also believed, as many of you do, that I didn't remember or wasn't good at the things we learned in high school because I didn't pay close enough attention or didn't work hard enough. I didn't remember a single book we had read in high school English, and I was sitting in the principal's office, explaining to a panel of very important school people why they should pay me twice as much as I've ever made in my life to "teach literature" to other people's children...and the last book I had read had been about tiling.

Gee whiz, Huskie, if you didn't pay attention in high school, didn't do well in college, are nervous around principals, and primarily fill your allotted reading time with books that have the words For Dummies *in the title, then why in the world would you waste your time, and your students' time, as a teacher?*

After my first semester at college I jumped into a car with

a bunch of guys and drove to a state park a half hour away. I can't remember if I knew what the mission was, but it was late at night and I was likely just going with the flow. The park was closed so we hopped over the fence and walked by moonlight to the edge of this very steep, very high cliff. I don't remember for sure, but I think there was a dozen of us, and the driver of the car I was in had a book bag full of textbooks. With the glee and fervor that must have been felt around Jack's *Lord of the Flies* banquet fire, he threw the books one by one over the cliff as we all whooped and danced on the stone wall; it's a wonder none of us fell to our deaths.

A couple decades ago it had seemed so logical. Of course he would want to destroy his textbooks. They were torturous and those classes sucked. I would have done the same thing, except I don't think I knew what we were doing when I first got in the car. Classes were over, we didn't need the books, and screw that school...we'd throw *it* down the cliff if we could.

I've never thrown my power tools down a cliff after finishing a project. I've never destroyed any books that I've acquired of my own volition, or sold them...in fact, I have boxes of books in my garage and basement that I *should* get rid of, but can't bring myself to do it. I've never had any ill feelings towards my garden. I've never had the urge to sell, throw away, or destroy anything that helped me complete something I intentionally chose to do. And I never once thought it was weird that I should feel excited, drunken joy in watching someone throw books over a cliff, or strange that I was excited to see how much money I could get for my college textbooks. It never occurred to me that that was odd.

Things I haven't thought about in years just kind of pop up. For example, I had standing rules in high school: I didn't do homework that I couldn't finish in homeroom or on the bus (I did all my homework at home once, and missed a tackle football game outside, and never made that mistake again); on principle I never read a novel assigned by an English teacher, even though I spent most of my early childhood in the library. I'd pick up enough in class discussion to do whatever assigned work, assuming I could finish the assignment in homeroom; since I got to school early, I would climb through windows and open teachers' doors to confuse them; I would take the building physically apart, whenever possible. I have no clear memory of any class, but many memories of the weight room and football, lunch, and the bus ride back and forth, the only parts of school I enjoyed. I *wanted* to care about what the teachers cared about, I *wanted* to give a damn about my grades, but I physically *could not* bring myself to do it.

This was the reason I wanted to become a teacher. As much as my feelings for school vacillated between indifference and hatred, I didn't see that anyone had any other options, and so I figured I could dedicate my life to lessening the suffering of our nation's adolescence. I would do only fun things with interesting material and change the face of school. The problem I failed to anticipate was that when I do fun and interesting things, I'm actually doing the things that I personally find fun and interesting, and while I can act like a clown and "engage" (optimistically) eighty five to ninety percent of my students, ultimately I'm only useful content-wise to students who were already interested in the content, and merely entertaining to some of the rest. For a small percentage each year, my class will be torture; who that percentage is will depend on the fun and interesting things *I choose* to do, but it's inevitable. I will torture some kids every year.

It took me a long time to realize this fact. No matter how loving, patient, and knowledgeable a teacher is, they will torture students with irrelevant, simplistic, and uninteresting nonsense.

Maybe you've noticed what I've noticed, and thought it strange, or dismissed it as youthful foolishness or that you were missing some critical piece of information that would reveal itself with age and wisdom – that is: every single teacher believes feverishly in the importance of the content of their class, and furthermore, believes that their assessment of you in their class is a direct measure of your capacity for future success, *while simultaneously not having a clue* as to the content of virtually any other discipline in the school. They will boldly state things like, *That's math, I'm an English teacher* or *That's literature, I'm a biology teacher,* practically admitting out loud that nothing learned in school is important (except, of course, the course they are teaching). I fell into this trap while tutoring at a student's home:

"Why are we doing this?" groaned the sixteen-year-old girl while reading a chapter from *To Kill a Mockingbird.* I hadn't yet had the heart to tell her that she was going to have to write, too.

"Because your teacher assigned it," I shot back.

"But whyyyy," she stomped her feet like a baby, which was funny to me because she had just had a baby less than a month before (hence the home tutoring).

I thought for a moment before giving her more of the canned stuff: "Because you have to do well in school to be successful in life. And this is what they're doing in school."

"Can't we work on chemistry? I like science." As a home tutor, I was responsible for all of the subjects.

"I just got your chemistry work today," I explained. "I need some time to look it over [google all the answers] before I can help you with it."

"You mean you don't know it?"

"I will," I said curtly, then smiled. "Let's just focus on English. Or history, if you want, I have something about trench warfare here. That could be fun!"

"Mister, are you successful in life?"

"Excuse me?"

"You don't know chemistry; you said I need to know this to be successful, so I want to know if you're successful. How much money do you make?"

"Uh- [shit! she caught me!]"

"How much? 'cause I'm not doin' this work if you make more than, like, a good amount."

This girl, who didn't know that hamburgers *or* chicken nuggets are made out of meat,[5] had left me totally speechless. For a moment. Then I remembered more platitudes. The ones about perseverance and doing things you don't like or want to do in order to build character and I *had* taken chemistry and I struggled but *that's* what made me successful and you won't like all of your teachers just like you won't like everyone in life and you'll have a boss one day and so on and so on. I bullied her into history handouts and, happily, neither of us had to think much for the next ninety minutes.

Two years later I was in a professional development (PD) and the topic was "Depth of Knowledge." "Depth of Knowledge" is a way of thinking about how "deep" you can go with information, a convenient hierarchy of smartness, e.g. remember, understand, apply, analyze, evaluate, and create. At the end of the PD, the instructor hands out a packet of old Regents exam questions from seven different disciplines, with about two multiple choice questions per discipline. The activity was to identify which sphere of smartness each question fell into (remember, understand, apply, create, etc.). It quickly devolved into everyone just trying to answer the questions. The facilitator didn't mind, but also didn't have any of the actual answers, so it turned into a fun game; a misprinted *Trivia Pursuit* that only had cards with questions. We answered the questions individually, and then came to a "correct" answer by consensus.

I got some questions right, but I answered "C" for a bunch because I figured the answer is usually "C." For the most part, the humanities folks got humanities questions

---

[5] We were reading *The Hunger Games*, and there is a scene where Katniss is hunting deer. "Eww," says the girl. "She eats deer? That's gross." "Well," I explained. "You eat cow, don't you?" "Ugg, cow, no way, disgusting!" "You don't eat hamburgers?" "Well, yeah, I eat hamburgers. Wait...that's cow?" "What did you think it was?" "Not meat! I thought meat was meat, vegetable was vegetable, and hamburger was hamburger! Wait – does that mean chicken nuggets were actually chickens?" "Kind of." "Ugggghhhhheewwwwwww I ate animals, that's so gross!" True story.

right, and the hard science folks did best in their discipline. With two exceptions: there was a math teacher who insisted that the statistics question didn't make sense, and a Social Studies teacher (our facilitator) who couldn't remember a U.S. History question because he currently taught Global History ("Man, I haven't taught U.S. in, like, four years"). At exactly that moment it dawned on me. I now had a completely different set of questions.

Take, for example, the "summer slide" – that thing when students know so much in May and June but by September have to learn it all over again, and teachers huff and puff and blame everything in the world: *why didn't your parents review your geometry over the summer? Why didn't your teacher last year teach this? Why can't you remember things from June? Why don't I ever get "good" classes?* Some of the braver teachers may even say something like, *this is why we need a twelve-month academic calendar*, although most people who say that are people who already work twelve-months.

If you ask a better question then you get a better answer. For example, *Why do we teach what we teach if we as instructors lose the knowledge within a year?* And I use the word *teach* very loosely when referring to *knowledge*, e.g. the disjointed, out of context, unimportant facts you might find in a trivia game. Just fine for a snowy winter night at home with the family, and even fun in a PD where absolutely nothing was at stake. *But what if our paycheck depended upon how much trivia we could answer (because their ability to graduate does)? What is the purpose of school? What's the point? Can you remember what was taught in high school? How much did it help you in college? How much has it helped you in your career? What are your fondest memories of high school?* Mine are of the bus ride back and forth, where I could talk and joke with my friends for nearly an hour; tormenting my homeroom teacher; lunch; football. There were some one-off things, like that one party I went to, climbing on the gym roof, throwing a dead frog into the drop ceiling in the lab because a girl dared me to (not so funny three late-spring days later, but hey, a girl dared me, what was I supposed to do?).

In fact, the only teacher I clearly remember was my trigonometry teacher. I hated him and he hated me. I answered in haikus on his homework to spite him. I drew on his tests to mock him. And he couldn't do a damn thing about it except fail me. My final *screw you* to Mister Whatshisface was a 96% on the trig Regents exam. It took me one weekend of practice test after practice test, and was easily my highest state exam grade ever.

I'm not suggesting that fiery hate be the thing that drives you, because that seems awfully unhealthy, but it was what drove me to rock that exam. I had focus and strategies *because* I had a purpose – I wanted to embarrass this guy. I wanted him to have to go to the principal and explain how he gave a 50% for each of the four quarters to a kid who scored a 96% on the Regents. I wanted him to know that I can learn trigonometry without him. I don't remember why we butted heads to begin with, but I wanted to have the final word in mid-June.

The use of the word "work" as it pertains to students was one of the first things I noticed after I became a teacher. "He's not doing my work," or "I can give him some work to make up for the past week when he was absent," or "If you do the work, you'll be fine [grade-wise, I assume]." Work hard and you'll be successful. Well, yeah, unless you are working hard painting green rocks yellow on Wednesdays and yellow rocks green on Sundays. I can do all the work for my Underwater Fire Preventionist Certification and even graduate top in my class.

I don't know trigonometry anymore. But I bet I could learn it, if I wanted to, and I bet I could go my whole life without knowing it and be fine. You could make a case for learning anything. Of course literacy is high on the list of things you should learn. Enough math to not get ripped off at the stores and to balance a checkbook is a requirement. I replaced my hot water heater with a bucket of tools, about $500, and a stubborn sense of self-reliance, my only other weapons foul language and Youtube.

So then, what should we teach? It's better to know than to not know, but if you choose one then you choose not to choose infinite others, which is in a sense inevitable, but as teachers and school staff and governments, we are choosing for other people; making decisions as to how they should act and what they should be and what kind of society *we* want, not what kind of life or society the student imagines.

In New York State public high schools, where I teach, a student is considered career- and college-ready when they complete 4 credits of English Language Arts, 4 credits of Social Studies, 3 credits of math, 3 credits of science, .5 credits of health, 1 credit of the arts, 1 credit of foreign language, 2 credits of physical education, and 3.5 credits of electives. They also must successfully pass five Regents examinations. All of which is very important and serious to the teachers who teach them and the State that mandates them. Yet quite often, they are not very important to the students who are being taught them, and that turns fine dining into being tied down and force fed, which in turn produces stupidity. For example, the K-12 math curriculum could be taught in eight weeks to almost any willing student[6] and any eighth grader could read thirty or forty good books a year, so long as they get to choose what to read.[7] The learner is the most important element in the learning process – it's shocking to me how this is a controversy – followed by their environment, followed by whatever instructor there may be. And when I say the learner is the most important variable, I don't mean to say that what is most important is how well a learner "listens," "follows directions," or "lives up to their potential." I mean their emotional and spiritual investment, as well as their personal decision for sustained concentration, in whatever work it is they are doing, determines how much they get out of any one thing. I mean it's their choice.

---

[6] *Just do the Math* by David Albert
http://www.besthomeschooling.org/articles/math_david_albert.html
[7] *The Reading Zone* by Nancie Atwell

After all of our basic needs are met, what we want more than anything is a sense of higher purpose – we need to know that we are important, necessary, and that our actions will have lasting effects. Generally, there are two ways that we find higher purpose. The first is by changing the external world to fit your view of a utopian society; the second is by changing yourself to become the world you'd want to live in.

Molding the external world to fit your view of utopia often necessitates you changing other people. This usually means you are going to force other people to do something or be something, with or without their consent, and punish those who don't conform or comply. The thing that you'd want to change in people may be "good" or "bad" by most reasonable standards, and the people may willingly comply or they may not, but it's still *your* thing, so you'll probably see it as good regardless of the level of buy-in, and justify unreasonable means to achieve it, e.g. place people under surveillance, jail them, fine them, or commit violence against them to enforce it. Finding a higher purpose by molding the external world is what we do when we enforce compulsory education laws (education is good) or when ISIS throws homosexuals off buildings to their death (homophobia and murder are bad). Obviously these aren't the same things – not even close – but they are both attempts at finding a higher purpose in something bigger than yourself by forcing your worldview on others.

Conversely, you can find a higher purpose by looking inside of yourself, and changing yourself as necessary to, as Mahatma Gandhi said, *be* the change you want to see in the world. Actually, Gandhi's exact words were:

We but mirror the world. All the tendencies present in the outer world are to be found in the world of our body. If we could change ourselves, the tendencies in the world would also change. As a man changes his own nature, so does the attitude of the world change towards him. This is the divine mystery supreme. A wonderful thing it is and the source of our happiness. We need not wait to see what others do.

Finding a higher purpose by looking inside yourself is what happens when you offer your writing or your wisdom up to the world (art and advice are good) or form a hate-group like the Westboro Baptist Church (speaking ill of dead soldiers and telling everyone they are going to hell is bad). There is nothing inherently good or evil about how you decide to find your higher purpose. You could do good or evil things whether your goal is other-people-improvement or self-improvement, however, I would argue strongly to consider the latter before considering the former. When you look to change the world for the better, whether the world wants to change or not, then you necessarily limit other people's ability to find what makes them important and necessary to this world. Do what brings you joy and purpose, but do it without expectation. *You have the right to work, but never to the fruits of your work. Don't engage in action for the sake of reward, and do not resign yourself to inaction.*[8]

It's easier to try to change other people or coerce other people to act in a way that you think right, than to live the kind of life that you wish the world would live. Think about how many people flock to causes that require them to change other people through compulsion; it's easier to justify almost any force necessary if you can convince yourself you are doing it for other people's good, e.g., killing the Indian to save the man.[9] No matter how good the intentions of finding self-importance through compelling others, you are still undermining a person's ability to do three things:[10]

1. Come to it willingly.

---

[8] *Bhagavad Gita*, Chapter 2, Verse 47

[9] "Kill the Indian, and Save the Man:" Capt. Richard H. Pratt on the Education of Native Americans

[10] I first read this in *The Making of a Moron* by Niall Brennan; 56 years later, Daniel Pink argues something very similar in his book *Drive: The Surprising Truth About What Motivates Us.*

2. Understand the purpose.
3. Have an opportunity for self-expression.

It's not to say that you can't have some of these things, some of the time, in an environment of compulsion. However, there is a far greater chance that a student could do all of those things in choosing to build raised beds and gardening, than a biology teacher assigning gardening as a requirement for graduation. The "thing" itself is not the issue. The issue is the social and emotional state of learner, and compulsion does not tend to breed contentment or happiness in humans. As Plato said, *Knowledge which is acquired under compulsion has no hold on the mind. Therefore do not use compulsion, but let early education be a sort of amusement; you will then be better able to discover the child's natural bent.*

The excessive triggers, safe spaces, and other emotional fragilities that seem to characterize this generation are a part of the negative emotions bred through compulsively demanding and valuing external things in school. We have as a society put a lot of effort into focusing on extrinsic things and very little effort in valuing intrinsic rewards. We have a society of individuals who do not understand themselves as individuals, and so they have a hard time understanding others or processing their own emotions.

We adults have a tendency to dismiss teenagers' temper tantrums; either by drawing attention to their underdeveloped prefrontal cortex or by comparing their problems with someone who has an even worse problem (stop whining about which value meal I bought you, there are starving people in China). I try to avoid making those types of comparisons. Perception is reality, so your problems are no less your problems just because there are worse problems out there, and there are always worse problems out there. However, I tend to agree with Robert Frost when he says, *Education is the ability to listen to almost anything without losing your temper or your self-confidence.* By this definition, I don't think anyone can claim that we are successfully educating this next generation.

5

COMPLACENCY PAINS

The summer of 2016 I contracted Lyme disease. Borrelia is a horrible bacteria that corkscrews into your cells. My symptoms were exhaustion, tingling in the hands and feet, brain-fog, chills, shivering like a newborn baby polar bear (even in ninety degree temperature), and a soreness in my neck and ribs that made me question whether I had been kicked by a horse and had forgot about it due to the brain-fog. I was on antibiotics and herbal medicines for a year, which devastated my digestive system. In a sense, I was lucky – some people battle with Lyme for decades. I learned two very important lessons from this experience.

First, my wife and I did as much research as we could on Lyme. Lyme is named after the city in which it was first discovered – Lyme, Connecticut – and not far from there is a place called Plum Island. On Plum Island was a military base which was converted into an animal disease center. The conspiracy theory is that Lyme disease was purposefully developed as a bioweapon to be used in jungle warfare, and that it accidently escaped on the wings of birds. That would sort of explain why so little money has gone into Lyme research for humans, although there are Lyme vaccinations for dogs, and how difficult it is to get a proper diagnosis, despite the ridiculous number of people who come down with this awful disease. In other words, the less poking around, the better. It also makes sense from my experience as a former soldier – Lyme rendered me completely combat-ineffective. It is a near perfect way to incapacitate troops, and the fact that it isn't generally lethal would further tie up logistical trains. Of course, the CIA could have airdropped Gameboys, cable television, and credit card applications to Che and his guerrillas, and based on what that's done to our society, it probably would have had the same effect as Lyme on *la revolución*.

The second lesson I learned was the danger of removing human judgment and wisdom from the practice of medicine. I hadn't had the classic "bulls-eye" rash that many Lyme patients get, I had never seen a tick on my body, and the most basic blood tests came back negative. I didn't meet the minimum requirements for a diagnosis, according to some damned flow chart. A day later I wound up in the emergency room, popping acetaminophen every three hours just to keep my body from shaking uncontrollably. I did a lot of my own legwork, found a specialist, paid a lot of money for a more advanced blood test, and finally got a diagnosis.

In the months leading to an official diagnosis, I felt as if I'd gone crazy. I knew it had to be Lyme – all the symptoms matched and I had recently been to an area where Lyme is rampant. However, before that official diagnosis, I was made to feel like I was "faking it." All of the tests had been negative, so I was embarrassed to even tell people I had Lyme, even though it is well known with Lyme that the basic tests only show a fraction of the strains, and even then are not wholly reliable. In a way, I was lucky my symptoms were so severe. Had they been mild, I would have taken my doctor's advice and just gone home and dealt with the pain with the assumption that that's what happens when you get to be the ripe old age of thirty-four. What's scary is that some people have been living with Lyme for decades and don't even know it, assuming that their years of misdemeanoring have finally caught up to them.

Most of us have a figurative Lyme disease. We are in pain all the time, and have come to the conclusion that this is just what life is. We have been sold on the idea that debt is a normal, healthy way of life. We have been sold that fast food is food, that variety in what we eat is unimportant, that frequent intoxication is a part of our culture, and so we build our bodies with poison. We have been sold on commercialism and the idea that things can fill the emptiness that comes in not knowing ourselves or our place in the world. *War is peace. Freedom is slavery. Ignorance is strength.*[11]

We have been sold by schools that we are stupid. We trust the standardized tests and the standardized teachers, and even when we tell people things like "I have test anxiety" or "I'm not book-smart, but I'm a genius on the dance floor, in theater, on the basketball court, etc.," a part of us feels like a liar, because unlike Lyme, there is no "advanced test" that we can pay a thousand dollars for to quantify our specific type of *special*, to prove to ourselves that we aren't crazy. Even when we score high on tests we still feel stupid, because we know that we don't retain the useless trivia beyond a summer vacation – we have been sold that our families don't have the capacity to educate us, and that anyone who falls to the left of the bell curve in a particular thing at a particular time should be medicated or held in the school building for longer periods of time, or come to the school system at a younger and younger age. We have been sold on bondage as freedom and we are in constant pain because of it.

I don't know if I believe that Lyme was manufactured intentionally by the government. I'm not much of a conspiracy theorist. However, the reason people find it plausible is because we all know that exhaustion and brain-

---

[11] George Orwell

fog are two great ways to keep people from fighting. The government doesn't need Lyme to do that to us. We do it to ourselves. We rationalize all of the unnatural things we do when we allow their *normal* to infect our decision making. There isn't just one battleground. I've mentioned debt, fast food, alcohol abuse, drugging little kids, and the culture of medical standardization, but I believe ground zero in the fight for personal freedom is compulsory schooling. We are fearful of an *Orwellian* world that *may be* while completely unaware of the *Huxleyian* world that we *live in*, and what better place to learn to not give a shit than school? Especially since what, how, and when to learn is dictated to you by a series of strangers who then rate you against your peers in all of those things that you never had the opportunity to agree were important, and you had no context for anyway. It's a perfect formula to raise generations with low levels of understanding and high levels of indifference. Those are just the kinds of people eager to consume student loans and credit cards, fast food, prescription medication, and mountains of junk.

How can we possibly say we are raising free-thinkers, risk-takers, adventurers, and lovers of freedom, when from ages five until seventeen we allow our kids to be raised out of our sight in a dictatorship? Then, for some reason, parents get a pit in *their* stomach when the teacher calls home?[12] That's unacceptable.

---

[12] *What does this teacher make? Me, frustrated.* Bruce Smith
https://writelearning.wordpress.com/2015/06/05/what-does-this-teacher-make-me-frustrated/

6

DIVERSITY

I got an e-mail from the Advanced Placement people giving me a heads up that I have "about ten African American, Latino, or Native American students" who are AP material (based on SAT & PSAT scores), and reminding me that this is a traditionally underrepresented group. Diversity has become one of those things that we all agree is important. If we thought about it, and threw all of our weight behind the "diversity is so much better than homogeny" tenet, then we'd have to admit that any Historically Black College would be better off with more white people, any school in Beijing would be better off with more Hispanics, and any all-girl school would be a much better place to be if only they had a couple dudes.

What do you think of when someone tells you, "It's a very diverse community" or "There's a lot of diversity at our school"? What about diversity do we find appealing? Having one of every shade and gender is great for the yearbook cover, but how does that otherwise benefit us?

When we say "diversity," we are usually implying racial or

ethnic diversity, but we should be focused on, and celebrating, diversity of quality thoughts, feelings, and experiences. From this perspective we are all diverse in some way. Racial or ethnic diversity is certainly one way to get to diversity of quality thought, but it isn't the only way.

In education, there is not much diversity of thought, but rather an inclination, an intuition, a *purpose* to standardize. School-people are an insulated bunch. Teachers go to graduate school where they are trained by former teachers, and administrators are former teachers who go to graduate school to be trained by former administrators who were former teachers, all with their own ideas of how to be successful in an outside world of which they were rarely a part. That particular plant is watered by the state, and so there's a clue as to who built this echo chamber, and to what end. Noam Chomsky said, "The smart way to keep people passive and obedient is to strictly limit the spectrum of acceptable opinion, but allow very lively debate within that spectrum."

Earlier this year I had a girl sigh loudly in my class, "Can't you just tell me what to do so I can do it?" It broke my heart. That's not learning or curiosity. It sure as hell isn't exciting, and it has no element of risk. There's no initiative. I mean, I could hit all the state standards, but she has been trained to wait for someone to tell her what to think and feel. That's not diversity.

Diversity is not possible in almost any school as a direct result of the relationship between the teacher and the students. I suspect there are two ways that school-people perceive a teacher's relationship with students: either the teacher views their students as clients, and attempts to meet the individual needs of the students; or the teacher views themselves as the students' boss who demands respect and compliance on the basis of the teacher's position.

The problem with viewing students as clients is that clients come willingly to a product or service and decide whether they buy or not, and businesses adjust what they offer based on the number of sales and the capacity and creativity of the business. In school, students aren't clients because there is no obvious or easy option to walk away from the product or service. Teachers, for their part, have responsibility without authority – that is, teachers do not have authorization to make any significant changes to what, where, who, or how they teach. This is why grades exist; as a stick and carrot to force a relationship that is otherwise unreasonable. Even school administrators largely lack anything but superficial authority over content or pedagogy; policy is determined by the school board (or some other governing body) and standards are dictated by the state and, increasingly, federal governments. So it's a business relationship that involves "clients" who don't have the authority to not purchase, and a "corporation" that can't adjust to the market, even if they wanted to. Viewing students as clients to be served is dishonest in the context of compulsory education.

Viewing teachers as a boss, similar to your first boss at a fast food restaurant, is a more honest perspective, and the lessons that are meant to be taught are for the most part analogous:[13]

- Stay where you are. You may not leave, you may not take initiative – you're a number (in most cases in schools, you are literally assigned an ID number and plugged into a master schedule).
- Work when it's time to work. Speak when it's time to speak. Be quiet when it's time to be quiet. Leave when it's time to leave.
- Surrender your will to the people in positions of authority. It doesn't matter if they are good, bad, or boring. They make decisions for you now.
- Authority figures decide what's important to do. You get no input in the matter except by the blessing of

[13] This list comes from "The Seven Lesson School Teacher", *Dumbing Us Down: The Hidden Curriculum of Compulsory Schooling* by John Taylor Gatto

school officials.

- Your worth is determined by the authority figure's assessment of you. That assessment will be some combination of how well you memorize trivia and how closely you conform to this list of rules.
- You are always being watched. If you deviate from the above set of rules, you will be written up. In a job you might be fired, but since schools have a hard time firing students, you'll more likely be reported to your parents. If your parents fail to hold you accountable to the above set of rules, then they too will be reprimanded.

These are the sorts of rules that are required in an entry level, assembly-line type of a job. You don't want a Value Meal by Committee, or an employee experimenting with the french fry grease. A compliant and predictable work force is necessary in these sorts of jobs. However, if job satisfaction is dependent on the worker freely choosing the job, understanding the purpose of what they are doing, and having the ability to express themselves in their work,[14] then it's safe to say that the job of pickle-station-guy is unlikely to be very rewarding.

If we are saying that the above bulleted "values" are important for students to learn because one day they will have a boss, then we must agree that the purpose of school is job training for shit jobs. We must also agree that we are spending all of this time and tax-payer money to train for jobs that people older than twenty-five typically don't have and that anyone could figure out with minimal training.[15] If this is what school is meant to instill, why not just let teenagers have minimum wage jobs for four years, then grant them a degree? At least then they'd get paid, and they'd learn the same things.

Who the hell started the *you need to do what your teacher says*

---

[14] Again, from *The Making of a Moron* by Niall Brennan and *Drive* by Daniel Pink

[15] http://www.bls.gov/opub/reports/minimum-wage/2015/home.htm

because you'll have a boss one day excuse for a compliance-based system of compulsory education? If I had a nickel for every teacher who echoed this sadistic myth, I'd be on a boat in the Caribbean instead of force-feeding seniors *Hamlet* (incidentally, if Hamlet were a senior in my class, and I told him to read Act 2 of *Hamlet* for homework, he'd give me the finger and poison my afternoon coffee). I think it's a valuable skill to, for example, think clearly and act calmly while in tremendous physical pain. That doesn't mean I think you should stick your tongue in an electric toaster six times a day, 180 days a year, for twelve years.

There's a meme out there that says *I don't know how to do my taxes or get a mortgage, but thank God I know Pythagorean's theorem.* Funny, and largely true, but also misses the point. Not everything worth doing or learning has a practical application. Singing, advanced math, and rock climbing are all valuable things that most people won't "use" in the same way they would "use" knowing how to change a tire; also, not everything useful could actually be taught in any one school or learned in any one lifetime. Almost anything is worthwhile if a young person puts their heart and sweat into it. The *you will have a boss one day* theory of education assumes that if we don't force students to read *Hamlet* or put salt on the french fries, then they won't, and that would be just terrible. *If we don't make them, they won't* might be the most damaging assumption school-people – and society in general – have about students.[16] The *you'll have a boss one day* theory is more honest than the *students are our clients* theory, but the former is a poisonous appeal to a single authority.

Public education will always be a political issue because it deals with a person's kids and money. Our federal government has run up double digits in trillions of dollars of debt, then turns around and writes the algebra standards for

---

[16] *Children don't like school because they love freedom* by Peter Gray
https://my.psychologytoday.com/blog/freedom-learn/200909/why-don-t-students-school-well-duhhhh

our kids. They can't figure out how to balance a budget, but they want to teach our kids calculus. There is no way any government can create *required* standards and then expect *innovative* results – and for what it's worth, the buzz word surrounding compulsory standards-based schooling is "rigorous." Rigor is what happens when a person dies, which is fitting since spending twelve years listening to adult strangers tell you what and how to learn will make you dead on the inside.

If we concede that different people are different, and that we value those differences, then creating standards of any kind will naturally benefit some over others. You are imposing a few dozen things. This naturally excludes any number of other things.

But Huskie, we need data-driven rigor to ensure college- and career-readiness with a laser-like focus on twenty-first century skills and change-agents to facilitate major initiatives to implement standards-based measurable growth and of course teacher accountability. You hear how vampiric many of these buzz-words sound, don't you? They want your children for their data and their soul. It has nothing to do with learning or nurturing. It certainly has nothing to do with making students better, passionate, interesting, curious, or diverse thinkers. Please don't be among the willingly-blind. Run.

If being a grenadier and later a teacher is apostolic, then who is doing the calling? If I'm the priest, then who is the church? These are narcissists, or incompetents, or missionaries, or some combination. They are taking our children and turning them into numbers, and assigning values to those numbers. Shame on us. If we allow the state to administer even a single compulsory test without opting our kids out, then we get exactly what we ask for.

I've had colleagues who have insisted that without a standards-driven government curriculum, there would be chaos. In other words, if the state didn't tell our children what to learn and how to behave, there would be violence in the street. That sounds like Thomas Jefferson's excuse for the obvious hypocrisy between his philosophy of freedom and his owning of humans: slaves are wolves that white people have by the ear, and that if we let them go then they will eat us and possibly each other. Pay close attention to those who have convinced themselves that they are the thin line between civilization and chaos. It's most helpful to play their rhetoric on a loop during Halloween to scare the kids.

Here is the crux of it: the state belongs to us, we don't belong to the state. The state exists to make things a little more convenient for us, not us to give them some purpose for existence. School belongs to us, not us to school. The moment they begin dictating to us what and how our kids will learn, what minimum "standard" our kids must reach to be blessed with their paper of approval, we have allowed students to be enslaved to a single metric. We are licking the hands of the institution that is taking more and more ownership of our kids from us, and taking more and more of what makes them unique from them.

7

NECESSARY VIOLENCE

I've seen refugee students, for summer Regents exams, scheduled for twenty-four-hours-worth of standardized tests, although I've never seen anyone actually sit that long. The record for what I've personally seen has been about sixteen hours – from around eight in the morning until midnight, coloring in bubbles and scratching out short answers on someone else's idea of an authentic assessment.

English Language Learners have six hours to complete each of their five Regents exams that are required for graduation in New York. Oftentimes, the tests that are required fall on the same day, which means they have to sit for ten to twelve hours of paper-and-pen tests in a language other than their own. I use the word *required*. There are no other obvious options but to walk out and fail. In my experience, approximately 25% to 50% of them will pass any given test, and when they fail, they take the test again. It's common for these teenage survivors of war to leave high school having taken well over a hundred hours of Regents exams; oftentimes this puts them in a holding pattern until they turn twenty-one-years-old.

Have you ever sat for twelve hours to fill in bubble sheets with your entire future on the line? If you did, was it consensual? Because twelve hours straight of non-consensual testing happens three times a year, every year. The only reason an adult would knowingly do this to any teenager, let alone one who is dealing with the trauma of war while at the same time trying to learn English, is self-preservation. The school needs to survive, so tough break, kid.

I understand that students need to learn, and international kids especially need to learn English, but again, when was the last time you, or anyone you know, sat for twelve hours of bubble-sheet testing? After these students graduate, drop out, or age out, when will they ever have to do that again? Can you think of any other possible way in the world to test for competency in English? A better, more authentic way? A humane way? If you suspected a parent was making their teenage son or daughter kneel and pray, or read sheet music, or watch game-tape, or do practically anything while holding still and not talking, for six to twelve hours a day, all for the privilege of being considered a "grown-up," then you'd call Child Protective Services. This is nothing less than legalized child abuse oversaw by adults who generally care, but are doing it in the name of a machine and have somehow rationalized themselves out of speaking up. To be more straightforward, teachers and administrators who bear witness to this accept their impotence in the same way cowards have done throughout all of history.

I've been told a couple of times that I have a professional and ethical responsibility to uphold the law, and to consider my personal integrity. Here's a dirty little secret: instances of cheating on exams are much higher within the refugee population. We catch them almost every year. That shouldn't be a shock. There's a breaking point when you lower the probability of achieving a task to virtually zero, at the same time raise the irrelevant bullshittedness of the task to a hundred, and all the while keep the stakes set at *your personal freedom.* If I told all of you that you had to memorize pi to thirty places by tomorrow, or else you lose your job or you're kicked out of college, or more aptly, be forced to add five years before retirement or a year before you can graduate college, then some of you dear readers would cheat.

I'm sick of hearing those words: *professional duty* and *ethical responsibility*. Using that same yard stick, Huck should have returned the slave Jim to his rightful, lawful owner. Instead, Huck decides to "go to hell." We teach *The Adventures of Huckleberry Finn* in our Advanced Placement Literature class – it's required, so presumably we're supposed to learn lessons from it. If challenging and opposing the state, and challenging and opposing those shoulder-shruggers and oh-it's-terrible-but-what-can-we-doers in our midst, means that I'm unprofessional, unethical, and am going to hell, then screw it, I'm going to hell. At least there'll be cursing.

It's worth restating that these kids who I'm referring to aren't delinquents or truants who fail tests due to lack of effort or other shenanigans. Many of them are kids who have come from war, who lived in refugee camps, who have seen and experienced things as children and teenagers that I'm still processing as a veteran who went through it as an adult.[17] They don't have resources like parents who speak English or a great understanding of our legal system. If you tell them that they need to sit for three tests at six hours each in a single day in order to "be successful" then they're going to do it, because they're running from the emotional trauma of war and exile toward an American dream that includes a high school diploma. They'll trust us and do whatever it is we tell them to do. And what we're telling them is they need to bubble shit in for the better part of a day straight. It's unconscionable and I'm nauseous to think I'm a part of it. I'll repeat: they were in school taking tests until midnight, and

---

[17] It's probably also worth noting, I was part of the occupation more-or-less by choice. I've known teenagers who, up until they landed in the U.S., have known nothing but war.

some version of this has been going on for years.

Here are some facts. The kids need the double time, six hours per test, or they won't finish. Regents exams are only offered at specific times on specific days. Students need five tests to graduate. If the district decides that students can only test for six hours on any given day (one test), then twenty-year-old seniors who need three tests to fulfill graduation requirements won't ever graduate. You can't fix this by rearranging dates or times because the problem isn't a test. Taking the position that you are "anti-test" means that you are anti-a-piece-of-paper. The problem isn't paper; any of us could write a test today that will never be used to abuse a child-survivor of war. The problem is compulsion.

I do not want to give some special testing exemption to refugees or other English learners; I offer the above as a personal anecdote that is an explicit example of how compulsory testing is harmful to students, but compulsory testing is harmful even to students who ace them. Compulsion is another word for slavery and I'll have none of it.

Is passing five Regents exams the only way we can assess readiness for adulthood? If it's not the only way, is it the best way? Has the New York State Board of Regents developed the perfect magical formula that, should you survive their little trivia game gauntlet, guarantees proficiency at adulthood? In New York and elsewhere, there are no clear public school options for students to move on with their life with some kind of credential, except for taking and passing other peoples' tests to other peoples' standards. Students applying to law school take the LSAT because they want to be lawyers. If they wanted to be doctors, they wouldn't have taken the LSAT, they would have taken the MCAT. Either way, they would have made the choice themselves.

Pro-freedom is a more sensible position than anti-test; the tests and what they do, as Gandhi put it, to our weakest members, are the symptoms of an obsession with homogenization and control. We need alternative pathways to a high school degree within the public school system that are not decrees from central planners. There are ways to become educated besides some arbitrary, rigid set of credits and tests.

Imposing a curriculum upon large groups of people, whether it be a single classroom or a nation, demands that the student relinquish their individuality, family, and culture; any nail that sticks up will get hammered back down. Since no two people are the same, there is no way a prescribed curriculum could equally respect the culture of any classroom larger than one student. This is the point Lt. Richard Henry Pratt, the founder and superintendent of the Carlisle Indian School, made in 1879: *We must kill the Indian to save the man.* I've heard similar arguments for compulsory pre-K. In order for kids to learn the *correct* way to read or do math, they must be removed from their families as early as possible and for as long as possible; or else, their "incorrect" family and culture will cause them to be *left behind.* Ergo, *No Child Left Behind.* Wisconsin v. Yoder (1972) argued in a similar fashion that the Amish could not possibly learn without going to school, and that if the Amish would not relinquish their kids then parents would be jailed. This is the quintessential violence perpetrated in the name of protecting families from themselves. While we're at the business of eliminating compulsory testing, we may as well eliminate compulsion from schools altogether.

Any sort of imposition of will of one person over another without their consent is a form of violence. I'm mainly referring to adults and young adults. Of course, we impose our will on our own biological children: when they run out into the street, eat too much chocolate, attempt to access questionable sites on the internet, etc. We imposed our will upon their spirit by bringing them into this world and slapping a name on them, all without their consent. It's an interesting debate as to how much freedom young children should be given. I don't claim to be the absolute authority on how much freedom kids should have. I do believe that parents and communities have more rights to kids than schools do, and that kids are sovereign humans who should have more rights than *read this book at this time and take this test with this math because it's good for you that's why.*

We could remove violence from a curriculum by cultivating students' natural interests, passions, and aptitudes. Sir Ken Robinson calls this *finding your element* and advocates for child-centered, individualized, custom curricula in public schools; such methods have worked for thousands, including the famous dancer Gillian Lynne, *The Simpsons* creator Matt Groening, and the President of the International Economic Association Dr. Paul Samuelson.[18] This is not a school without curriculum; this is an education in which individuals are respected enough to create their own curriculum in collaboration with teachers who act as mentors. This is the concept behind Michelle Jones's Wayfinding Academy in Portland, Oregon. Wayfinding Academy is a two-year college in which students, in collaboration with staff, develop their own course of study and direct their own learning. It would be a more peaceful and harmonious way to run a society, but one that would render compulsion in schooling and testing obsolete.

Even if the tests were great – that is, that test results were some kind of indication of knowledge or ability – I'd still be vehemently anti-compulsion. It's the principle of consent that drives me, not the paper itself; however, if truth be told, standardized tests by the nature of their standardization can only ever be narrow in scope and superficial or mechanical in content. Albert Einstein said:

> *I am opposed to examinations – they only deter from the interest in studying. No more than two exams should be given throughout a student's college career. I would hold seminars, and if the young people are interested and listen, I would give them a diploma.*[19]

---

[18] *Finding Your Element*, Sir Ken Robinson
[19] *The Ultimate Quotable Einstein*, 2013

Perhaps part of the problem is that we take these tests when we're teenagers, back when we have no political or social clout, and then we put them out of our mind for the rest of our lives. I argue that questions on standardized exams, even high-stakes exams such as the Regents exams that are required for high school graduation, are most of these things:

- **Uninteresting:** Although subjective, I maintain that most questions on standardized exams are just plain boring. Has anyone ever completed a three-hour exam and left saying to themselves, "Huh. I wonder if the library is open so I can go learn more about what was discussed in passage 2?"

- *Internally* **and** *externally* **disconnected:** It's a crapshoot whether or not a student can connect to a question – for example, if a poem about an Asian father disappointing his son means anything to the student with the #2 pencil. It's never the case that more than a few questions will have anything at all to do with the subsequent few questions, other than they are all under the general heading of "English Language Arts" or "World History."

- **Inherently close-ended:** There is only one right answer for each multiple choice question. There is no opportunity to explain the rationale behind an incorrect answer, nor is there an opportunity to discuss things a student might *know* about a particular subject if they happen to *not know* the answer to the test designer's question. In other words, I might know a dozen things about the modernization of Japan, but not the one thing that was asked on the World History Regents (by the way, the answer to the "modernization of Japan" question is always "westernization", so just circle that). It's not much better with short answers and essays. Whether we teachers grade on a two-point scale, a five-point scale, or a six-point scale, our valuation is almost always the same or within a point of each other. There are specific things that the student can do to achieve four out of six, or five out of six, or to be scored no higher than three out of six. This is the illusion of open academic discourse.

- **Therefore, unimportant:** Nothing that is uninteresting, disconnected, and close-ended could possibly be important. Reading poetry or understanding how plants grow can be important, no doubt – but when ripped from context and crammed into a little *make your mark heavy and dark* box, it is magically transformed into something best memorized for the test, and forgotten soon after.

- **Lacking consent:** I personally don't see much value in the SATs (and colleges are gradually understanding this, too),[20] but nobody is forcing anyone to take them, either. If you want to, you may, and if you don't, then you won't. Colleges likewise are free to require them as a prerequisite to admissions, or not. Any test that requires a passing rate for graduation within the context of compulsory schooling is blatantly violent – the demand is to relinquish your freedom and your opportunity for individual expression, complete someone else's task for someone else's purpose, and your failure to adequately complete our goal that we've set for you will result in another year of lockup. You may not leave the school building until you pass my tests or exceed twenty-one-years of age.

In the spirit of being arbitrary, I selected the Algebra Regents to use as an example (based on its alphabetic position.) I randomly selected the first three questions of the

[20] According to *Fairtest*, http://www.fairtest.org/university/optional

exam to test my five hypotheses. You could do the same with just about any question from any standardized test, and I'm confident you'll come to similar conclusions:

1 Which expression is equivalent to $16x^2 - 36$?

   (1) $4(2x - 3)(2x - 3)$ (3) $(4x - 6)(4x - 6)$

   (2) $4(2x + 3)(2x - 3)$ (4) $(4x + 6)(4x + 6)$

2 What is the solution set of the equation $(x - 2)(x - a) = 0$?

   (1) -2 and a (3) 2 and a

   (2) -2 and $-a$ (4) 2 and $-a$

3 Analysis of data from a statistical study shows a linear relationship in the data with a correlation coefficient of -0.524. Which statement best summarizes this result?

   (1) There is a strong positive correlation between the variables.

   (2) There is a strong negative correlation between the variables.

   (3) There is a moderate positive correlation between the variables.

   (4) There is a moderate negative correlation between the variables.

Algebra I (Common Core), January, 2017

- **Uninteresting:**
  - For items one and two, some people may find it fun and rewarding to solve algebraic expressions or to solve solution sets, but some people don't. There are no obvious reasons to learn how to answer these items, except that you might find it neat to play with.
  - For item three, most people should probably know what a correlation is, and have some concept of what a "strong" or "moderate" correlation implies, but you don't actually

have to know any of that to know that "-" means "negative" and that ".5" is a midpoint, or "moderate."

o Each of these items are so easy that they border on ridiculous – for question one, none of the answers have signs that, when multiplied, could equal a negative number, except answer two. You could answer item two if you understood the concept that zero multiplied by anything equals zero. Item three isn't much more than a vocabulary question – if you know what the words "correlation" and "moderate" mean, and you know that "negative" is represented by "-" and you know that ".5" is in between a 0 and a 1, then you'll know the answer.

- *Internally* and *externally* **disconnected:**
  o Algebraic expressions have no obvious connection with determining the strength of a correlation.
  o None of those things have anything to do with anything most people need to know or do, except if they were to choose to do it for fun.

- **Inherently close-ended:**
  o There is one correct answer for each of these questions. There is no opportunity for explanation or for further application. The answers are 2, 3, and 4. Thank you, and have a nice day.

- **Therefore, unimportant:**
  o You don't have to know anything to answer these questions, except that a positive multiplied by a negative is the only way to multiply and get a negative, that zero multiplied by any number is zero, and what

the words "correlation" and "moderate" mean. Therefore, technically speaking, this is senseless, stupid shit.

- **Mutual consent:**
    - ○ This test is a requirement for graduation – we will not ask you for your consent. You will remain in the school building until you pass this test or turn twenty-two-years-old, whichever comes first.
    - ○ Although these questions are idiotic, more than a third of all New York students failed this exam. Shocking, considering the pressures on teachers to prepare students, and the consequences to students for not passing. You can assume what you wish, but I don't believe a third of our state's kids are morons. Plato said, "Knowledge that is acquired under compulsion obtains no hold on the mind." The Sudbury School teaches to proficiency the K-12 math curriculum in merely eight weeks to almost any willing student.[21] "Learning can only happen when a child is interested. If he's not interested, it's like throwing marshmallows at his head and calling it eating."[22] This isn't some new-age, hippy-dippy, permissive, irresponsible nonsense. It's literally the only way people can effectively learn, and we've known this for at least 2,400 years.

Not everything on every standardized test is completely without merit, although I couldn't think of a better way to ruin a love of learning than ripping facts from context and

---

[21] *Just do the Math* by David Albert
http://www.besthomeschooling.org/articles/math_david_albert.html
[22] Katrina Gutleben

forcing students to recite those facts under duress. Some of the passages from the New York English Regents, the test I score, are actually really good, and if you're lucky, really funny in the context of the test. For example, the August 2014 exam contained a passage from Mark Twain's *Life on the Mississippi*, and the main idea was something like *the more you learn about something, the less beautiful and magical it becomes,* concluding with a paragraph sympathizing for doctors who can no longer look at a blushing beauty without thinking she is coming down with something contagious.[23] The January 2015 exam contained an excerpt from *Walden*, in which Thoreau details his escape from a life of societal expectations that he deems to be a life not worth living at all, just as a student might withdraw from compulsory schooling in order to live their dreams. It's as if the test writers actually have a sick sense of humor, or else they are completely devoid of any self-awareness. Grace Llewellyn wrote in her book *Guerrilla Learning:*

> *For information to have meaning, there must be meaningful context for the information. Information without a context is not actually information at all but data. For example, a computer stores data, but it doesn't understand the data. For the data to become information, a human being has to get involved.*

Test-takers aren't performing human tasks. They are performing data-dumps.[24] The problem with assessing

---

[23] Irony is defined as these lines on a standardized test: "Now when I had mastered the language of this water, and had come to know every trifling feature that bordered the great river as familiarly as I knew the letters of the alphabet, I had made a valuable acquisition. But I had lost something, too. I had lost something which could never be restored to me while I lived. All the grace, the beauty, the poetry, had gone out of the majestic river!"

[24] *My Kids Are Straight A Students and They Know Nothing* by Kevin Kruse http://www.forbes.com/sites/kevinkruse/2017/01/13/my-kids-are-

students *en masse* at school is that the more quantifiable the test, the more algorithmic the types of questions, whereas the less quantifiable the question, the more opportunity for creative and meaningful expression, but the more challenging the answer will be to grade. For example, if I asked you to list the capitals of the states, or solve for *x*, or describe how the tone contributes to the theme, then I am asking strictly quantifiable questions. You can get them right or wrong, and if I ask you five questions and you answer three correctly, then you receive a 60% on the exam. The two pros of quantifiable questions are: though arbitrary, you could argue that capitals and *x*es and tones are good things to know (as are most things that go untested); if there is only one correct answer, and students are assessed consistently on whether or not they know that one answer, then there is a sort of fairness (if you ignore the lack of consent in compulsory school).

Other questions, such as *if god exists everywhere and in everything, then is the worship of things the worship of idols, or of god,* or, *how would you make a million dollars in thirty days,* or, *if for some reason the Civil War was not an option in 1861, what would have been the next best option to free the slaves, and would it have been more or less effective than war,* are all questions that invite creative and perhaps meaningful consideration, but are not easily quantifiable – any attempt to evaluate the quality of the responses would probably necessitate a rubric, would definitely be a disincentive for students to give risky answers, and, while some answers have more merit than others, suggesting that one answer to any of those questions is 60% correct while another is 82% is arbitrary and frankly silly.

In school, we generally prefer the former to the latter, because our system is built on competition with each other, so there needs to be an illusion of fairness. Also, we're data-driven, so we need to sort masses of individuals by various groups and numbers, and make sweeping data-based decisions for everyone's kids. We'll sometimes give questions

---

straight-a-students-and-they-know-nothing/#6bf7c094325e

that sound like they are inviting creative thought, but ultimately there's the issue of fairness between students, which means there needs to be a consistent way of grading, which naturally narrows the scope of possible answers and the willingness for the student to take creative risks. In school, we also seem to have fallen in love with the word "accountability," which can roughly be translated as "all you students and staff have no choice but to comply or be punished."

I'd like to offer a sincere question of my own: *Is it ever morally justified to cheat on school work or an exam?* I said *ever*. If I told you that you had an hour to memorize pi to twenty-five places, and failure to do so would result in a death sentence, would you be justified in cheating? Only a psychopath would say no. Strictly as a hypothetical, if you and I *mutually consented* to play a crazy game of, "memorize pi to twenty-five places in an hour and I'll give you a million dollars; fail, and you'll be put to death," then there is at least the moral argument, "they are both consenting adults choosing to enter into a messed-up contract, of their own free will." Of course, in school, virtually nothing is consensual.

I'll admit that's an extreme example. How about, a student spends from eight in the morning until three in the afternoon in classes she never asked for and doesn't want, only to spend three hours at rehearsal for a play she actually is passionate about, and upon getting home at six-thirty or seven at night, has the options of:

1. spending time at dinner with her family, but failing to complete two hours of homework and risking suspension from drama and a possible repeat of the school year, or
2. doing two hours of homework, but over time risks losing or damaging relationships with family, or
3. googling the answers and completing the homework in fifteen minutes, keeping the lead role, passing the academic year, and strengthening the bond with her

family.

Which is the more moral answer?

That question was too easy, so here's another: *Is it ever the case that it would be immoral to* not cheat *on school work or an exam?* In other words, would there ever be a time where a failure to cheat would be a personal failure and an indication of a weak, flawed character? If we're using the word "cheat" to mean "to violate the rules dishonestly," then would there ever be a time, as a teacher or a student, that your failure to violate the rules would be a reflection of your lack of integrity? I'd argue that there is some threshold where when a rule or law itself reaches a certain level of immorality, it becomes immoral to not break that rule or law; or, as Martin Luther King, Jr. said:

> I *submit that an individual who breaks a law that conscience tells him is unjust, and who willingly accepts the penalty of imprisonment in order to arouse the conscience of the community over its injustice, is in reality expressing the highest respect for law.*

Of course, by King's reckoning, perhaps what we need is a cabal of tenured teachers who decide to give all of their students 100% on their report cards, no matter what, and who then stand by the consequences of their actions.

For those of you unmoved by hypotheticals, I'll give a specific, real-life example (there are some exceptions to some of these points, but they are true enough):

1. In New York, it is required by public schools that students pass five Regents exams with a 65% or higher in order to graduate.
2. Failure to achieve this results in a repeat of the academic year, every year, until the tests are passed or the student surpasses twenty-one-years. I've known students who are in high school for six or seven years

because of these tests.

3. We have students who arrive to this country as teenagers who do not know any English, or who are in the process of learning English. In my district, many of those kids are refugees.

4. They get "double time," or six hours, for each test they take. It's common for students to sit for twelve hours straight of testing, in a language other than their own, to answer questions about antifederalists, dynamic equilibrium, and the narrator's central idea, with their freedom on the line.

5. In a nutshell, students who do not speak, or are learning, English, who are unfamiliar with our culture, are forced to sit for twelve hours straight, to answer algorithmic questions (the answer to many of which are a google search away), and failure on any one of these exams carries the consequence of not being authorized to leave school for an additional year.

You are a teacher, watching this unfold before you. Could you make the case that the rule itself is unethical? That *any* student, but particularly those at such an academic disadvantage as our immigrant and refugee population, who is forced to pass an exam under penalty of an additional year of detainment by the school, is being violated? If a law violates a person's liberty, is it not our duty to disobey? Is it not your ethical responsibility to act? Did you not join this profession to help and serve kids? Is it not a personal failure for you to shrug and say, "It's terrible, but what can you do?" and continue watching teenage survivors of war struggle with irrelevant factoids, twelve to eighteen hours at a clip, their very freedom on the line? How many of us have read history, and shook our heads and puffed our chest, and said, "If I were alive during *that* period, I would never have done *those* things to those people!"

Yet here we are, doing those things to those people.

8

THE COURAGE TO LOVE

You probably remember El Chapo.[25] He's a drug lord who has people on five continents; he and his men are responsible for over a thousand murders; he's built air conditioned tunnels between Mexico and the United States through which he ran a tremendous volume of marijuana, cocaine, and heroin; he owns politicians in Mexico and elsewhere; and even though he's in prison now, he's broken out of jail before.

Let's make believe he escaped again. This time, he's hiding in a house on your block – right now, this moment, El Chapo is close enough to you that he might complain if you play your music is too loud. He's a dangerous man, so the Mexican government sends a helicopter full of a dozen Special Forces soldiers and a couple of unmanned drones for close air support. The drones fire their missiles, the Special

---

[25] *Standing in Refugees' Shoes Scary Experience* by Brian Huskie
http://www.timesunion.com/tuplus-opinion/article/Commentary-Standing-in-refugees-shoes-scary-10959499.php

Forces mop up, and the drones fire more missiles to cover the soldiers while they extract. They kill El Chapo and level a city block while they're at it. Your house is destroyed and your six-year-old daughter is killed; twenty parents, grandparents, and other children are also killed.

Let's also pretend that El Chapo's henchmen are still scattered throughout the United States, which they probably would be. This is a threat to Mexico's national security, so they send drones with bombs and occasionally soldiers for fifteen years. That is, for the next fifteen years, every single hour of every single day, Mexican war machines are attacking cities and towns in the United States. Mexico is also funneling weapons and money to rival drug cartels in the United States to help fix the El Chapo problem (long after El Chapo was killed). Eventually, some Americans flee to Mexico, where their wives and husbands and children and parents won't be drone-bombed to death. In the process, two Americans with Mexican green cards are unjustly detained by Mexican authorities at *Aeropuerto de Guadalajara*. The Mexican people are outraged! They all wear the same colored t-shirt, protest at airports, and demand more Americans become Mexican citizens!

And there you sit, atop the smoking mountain of rubble that was once your home, covered in gray dust, cradling the mangled corpse of your little girl in your arms, looking south to a Mexican people who, in solidarity with you, have stopped riding Uber.

We have chosen not to address the issue of refugees head on. The United States admitted less than 90,000 refugees in 2016, half of whom were Christian, while simultaneously engaging in a foreign policy over the course of fifteen or sixteen years that has created millions of Middle Eastern refugees. So whether we grant zero refugees asylum, or grant a million, it's all just an effort to put a toothpaste cap on an open fire hydrant, while completely ignoring the person opening the hydrant. We support refugees in Albany, New York, because they are here and because we can't undo the wars that have happened. But my consistent message to all of you is peace – our country has been at war for a decade and a half. If we stopped doing the things that make people flee their homes in terror, then we wouldn't have to argue over how many refugees ought to be allowed in this country.

I find it easy to love my students. In the early years I had a special kind of love for the Iraqi students in my class, and in time that expanded to all the different refugees, and now I feel love, without effort or expectation, for all of my students. The English language has more words than any other language on earth, but only one word for love. I hope the love I have for my students is the unconditional love that Jesus had for all of God's children, but it's probably the kind of love that desperately wants to right the karmic scales, with the torn bodies and crumbled buildings on the other side.

You don't get it. I've been living in that world for a while – if I think about it, *I don't get* pre-Iraq Brian. He's a stranger to me. There isn't a neat little anecdote that expresses how differently you start to see the world, except maybe the time I was in the office at work and the stapler kept jamming, and, cursing, I told the other high school English teachers how this one time I was in a convoy, and we had to take a U-turn. My truck didn't have a gunner, and as it happened when we made the turn, a civilian car came out of nowhere and sped right toward me. We had been hit with a few car bombs recently, so I leaned out of the window with my M-4, aimed at the driver, and pulled the trigger. Nothing happened. The catch on the magazine had worn down and it wasn't seating properly in the weapon, but I didn't know that. I slapped the magazine, aimed, and squeezed again, with no result. At this point I figured we were dead, so I just kept slapping and squeezing like a maniac when, as if by a miracle, the car veered off to the side of the road and stopped. There were two young men in the car, dressed as Iraqi police, shaking and hyperventilating. *As it turned out, they just didn't see us, so no harm-no foul,* I said while laughing, slapping and squeezing the stapler like a madman. Apparently nobody else in the office got the joke.

Grandpa said that when he was in the Navy, Marines released everything when they died. An Iraqi Army convoy got hit, and our medic tried to save one of the wounded, but he died, naked. I saw it happen, and I expected him to shit all over the butcher's table, but there was nothing. Doc just cursed himself, as if it were his fault, and poured the mess into a bag. Later, I had a dream that he shit.

I've had other dreams, some of them based on real events, others complete lies my subconscious tells me. One mission I've dreamt about so many times, I no longer know what really happened. In one dream, I have a detainee and protect him from incoming mortar rounds; then I am alone, and everyone else is lost or dead; then I raid a house, pull the man out, and I hold my gun to his head while his kids watch MTV; then I am sitting on a slide guarding a mulch pile, while they kill my son under the monkey bars. In a dream it takes a thousand pounds of pressure to squeeze a trigger, and your legs never work.

There are other things that aren't dreams, like the piled-up bodies after a car bomb, and the bloody handprint and brains on the pockmarked wall of the crumbling building. I probably slept two hours in three days, and when I woke up I was screaming. Nobody seemed to notice, since none of them had slept, either. Sandbags had to be filled, and guard shifts had to be pulled. Maybe you won't get it, but this is how I've learned what love means. It's a decision you make, and there is nothing else remotely as important as this decision, but it takes courage. Like MLK said, *hate is too great a burden to bear.*

I didn't understand – and I mocked – the author Tim O'Brien when he wrote in *The Things We Carried*: "I was a coward. I went to the war." I was ready to kill for god and country, and O'Brien's notion that running to Canada was the *brave* thing to do was ludicrous to me. But it's not that going to war or not going to war makes you a coward. You are a coward when you betray yourself. You're also a coward if you aren't willing to go to war with your own deeply held beliefs, to challenge them, to wrestle with them until you come to a place where you can live with yourself – so that you know whether you are betraying yourself or not. It's said that the longest journey you'll ever make is from your heart to your head.

What a small and petty thing schools are, that make teenagers who have seen much more war than I have, take twelve or eighteen hours of standardized tests in a day, and tell them they can't leave the system until they pass all five tests. They've had experiences that you couldn't conceive – family members beheaded, car bombs, villages destroyed, families separated for years or decades or forever, a lifetime in refugee camps, community members killed and others committed to insane asylums. How pathetic we are that we allow refugee students to take tests that we know they will fail, and watch them come back, and fail, and come back, and show courage in the face of silliness. If you are a part of this system, and you don't speak out against it, then it's one of two things: either you believe deeply in the value of high-stakes, standardized tests, or, like I said before, you're acting like a coward. I don't mean that with any meanness or ill will. Courage is a high quality *fuck that* that results in a tar-and-feathering. You're not courageous for speaking out against Nazis, unless you are currently living in Nazi Germany. You are courageous when you look at the people you love, who believe or tolerate something that's clearly wrong, and you say *I love you, but no, I'm not doing it.* Let's be the people who were for Abolition *before* the Civil War.

Dropping out of school, not because you're a loser and you have no plan, but because you have a better plan than spending years of your life in a weird cycle of data uploads and downloads without ever learning anything, is a tremendous act of courage.

Any young person, grades seven to twelve, could break free of school and complete a self-prescribed course of study that would leave them fuller, happier, and better prepared than most any school could, but it would take courage to do so. If three or four or a dozen young people banded together, and decided to drop out of school and together put themselves through their own individualized program, superior by any measure to that of schools, then not only would they be demonstrating uncommon courage, it would likely be a declaration of war. Taking control of your own destiny is a courageous act of love, as well as revolution.

PART TWO:
A LETTER TO MY TEENAGE SELF

When I heard the learn'd astronomer,
When the proofs, the figures, were ranged in columns before me,
When I was shown the charts and diagrams, to add, divide, and measure them,
When I sitting heard the astronomer where he lectured with much applause in the lecture-room,
How soon unaccountable I became tired and sick,
Till rising and gliding out I wander'd off by myself,
In the mystical moist night-air, and from time to time,
Look'd up in perfect silence at the stars.

~Walt Whitman

9

CONSCIOUS SCHOOLING

I would never criticize a family for *choosing* public or private school over homeschooling. I'm advocating self-direction as the most peaceful, respectful form of educating, and while I think the student should have a say, it really ought to be a conversation between the parents and the child. Children should have some say in how they live their life, but how much of a say that is will depend on many things. Since my experience is mainly with teenagers, I would caution parents against assuming their teenage children are too immature or not self-motivated enough to withdraw from school and complete an independent, self-designed program. I would also caution homeschooling parents against dogmatically forbidding their teen to go anywhere near a high school. There are a lot of problems with compliance-based education – however, it would be foolish to suggest schools have absolutely nothing to offer, although as more and more learning centers and programs are developed, compulsory school will be rendered less and less relevant.

The problem is a complete lack of dialogue and intentional

decision making – in fact, going to school is rarely a *choice* at all, but rather just the thing you do because everyone else does it. There is nothing wrong with going into a school wide-eyed to where schools fall short, but making a conscious decision to use school where it benefits you, and to not take the insidious parts of school seriously. If you don't care about grades, then they can't use grades to control you or undermine your love of learning; if you shrug off homework, they can't continue to steal your time away from your family and community. There is also nothing wrong with parents supporting a teenager in withdrawing from school and allowing them to educate themselves – not in isolation, but by their own design. There are as many ways to get an education as there are people on earth, and contrary to popular school-lore, you don't need to be a certified expert to do it. The cornerstone to all of this is family dialogue and mutual respect for each other. Personally, as a parent, it's been my experience that I never know if I'm doing it right. None of us do, and it's likely none of us will ever know if we made the right decisions in raising our children, but we all want what's best for them. Listen, be open, and do your best to support your child in the best way you know how.[26]

There are rarely-used, but effective, methods for taking an education,[27] and I outline some of them in the next chapters, but first, some caveats:

- The tenth amendment of the constitution states that

---

[26] *Too Soon Old, Too Late Smart* by Gordon Livingston; Chapter 26 "Parents have a limited ability to shape children's behavior, except for the worse."

[27] "Nobody *gives* you an education. If you want one, you have to take it. Only you can educate you—and you can't do it by memorizing. You have to find out who you are by experience and by risk-taking, then pursue your own nature intensely." John Taylor Gatto, http://www.yesmagazine.org/issues/learn-as-you-go/take-back-your-education

all things not mentioned in the constitution automatically become the responsibility of the states. This includes education – technically, the states don't have to have a public education system at all, although all of them do, and constitutionally there probably shouldn't be a federal department of education, although there is. My lens is New York, and so those are the laws I am most familiar with, but I'm not a lawyer, and even if I were, laws change. I'm not against breaking an unjust law (most of us are felons anyway),[28] but it would behoove you to know what you are up against before you act.

- Resistance to compulsion in education is really only effective in public schools, in that a private school has the right to expel you. This is fair, I think, since you aren't forced by law to enter a private school – you (or at least your parent) consented for you to be there under agreed upon conditions.

- If you choose to stay in school, it's usually the case that schools have a legal standing to censor you if you use any of their resources, including teachers or anyone else employed by the district. There may be staff who are sympathetic to your cause; e.g., being active and vocal about methods of retaking your education – there is likely at least one who would like to help. I know I would. However, if they help you in any way, even after school or at the coffee shop on a Saturday, that will likely become a *de facto* "school activity," and schools have the right to control what goes on in school activities.

- If you plan to go to war to retake your right to choose what goes in your head (and I hope you do), it's going to be an uphill battle. You are going to be tested in ways you never thought possible, but whether or not you "pass" those tests, you will have begun your

---

[28] *Three Felonies a Day* by Harvey A. Silverglate

journey and will have learned something about yourself. I am going to detail the benefits of forming a small group so you don't have to go it alone.

- Know your rights, and never resort to violence. Schools, like most government agencies, know how to deal with violence. Riots, armed revolutions, and schoolyard brawls with school officials, are unlikely to do anything except put you in jail and undermine any moral high ground, not to mention that violence always begets violence. We are trying to take the violence inherent in compulsion out of schooling, not make the place physically unsafe! While government agencies know how to deal with violence, they have no defense against nonviolent resistance. Saying *no* in an environment where compliance is valued above all else is the most powerful thing you can do. Never resort to violence, but if you have a feeling things are about to turn violent, take out your phone and start recording!

Never lose focus. You are for peace and love, you are for individual sovereignty, you are for family and community, you are for your most basic right as a human to follow your heart and to choose your path. These things will naturally pit you against schooling, and you will have to fight, but any imbecile can complain and throw temper tantrums. It takes strength to lead the world towards a better tomorrow, and to continue to lead, even when it feels like there is nobody following.

10

FORM A *JUNTO*

When you are in school, do you feel as though the work that you do is important?[29] Is it meaningful to you? Does your homework help your community, or improve society? Do you feel a sense of risk, danger, or hardship in anything your teacher assigns or assesses you on (not to be confused with drudgery and anxiety)? Does school give you a personal sense of purpose and meaning? Or are you bored and complacent?

Our genetic programming is incompatible with modern schooling. Some of the most ideal conditions in which our genetic programming resonates is an infantry platoon in combat, or a sports team. I've done both of those things, and although I love peace and am intellectually against our current wars, I can testify that something about being in combat

---

[29] The Joe Rogan Experience #975,
https://www.youtube.com/watch?v=W4KiOECVGLg; the specific clips I reference: http://brianhuskie.com/2017/06/23/joe-rogan-experience-975-sebastian-junger/

spoke to me at a primal level. I'm certainly not alone. Talk to any combat veteran, and they'll tell you about the feelings of loneliness and isolation that accompanies returning to "normal," and the feelings of belonging, purpose, and a deep brotherhood that accompanied combat.

I can say the same thing about playing football, which I did in some form or another for fifteen years. You are important; the work you do matters; you are fighting to survive, and even more importantly, you are fighting for each other's survival. There is purpose and meaning behind your actions, and your actions are how you are judged and respected by your peers. These are extremely powerful and addictive experiences because this was how we as a species survived for tens of thousands of years, and evolution does not change our genetics as quickly as we change our society.

You aren't important to the school community, and the work that you do there doesn't matter. You know that as well as anyone else. If you transferred schools, dropped out, or graduated, the school will not be better or worse. The buses will still arrive, the bells will still ring, the lessons will still be taught, and students will still continue to do their best to remember the answers until the test, at which point the information will be purged from their minds. Your grades are "important" until the moment you get into college, and from that point on they are entirely meaningless. You are responsible for nothing more than what the teacher tells you to do. It is an incredibly safe and dull environment.

Even the phrase "school community" is a misnomer. Students are competitors with one another. They compete for grades and class rank, as well as for the affection and approval of the teacher; group work during normal school hours is typically superficial and met with groans from students, who are concerned primarily with their own grade and not with other students' learning. This is not how we are genetically wired to interact with each other in a community. If for tens of thousands of years our group of between 40 and 250 humans were in constant competition with one another, we would have gone extinct long ago. The school environment cannot resonate with our biology in the same way that, ironically, many afterschool sports and clubs do.

I'm not suggesting that we start drafting kids into the military, or make participation in sports compulsory. I do posit that humans are a learning species – it's how we survived for as long as we have – and to effectively teach and learn we need to be able to replicate some of the conditions in which we were programmed to learn. We can't pit students against each other with grades and expect authentic learning communities. Boredom is much more serious than "teenagers being teenagers" – twenty thousand years ago nobody found figuring out how to keep their clan alive "boring." Boredom is a deadly disease – literally. Read what Sebastian Junger says in Joe Rogan's interview:

> *The irony about modern society is that it has removed hardship and danger from everyday life, and it's in the face of hardship and danger that people come to understand their value to their society, and they get a sense of meaning from that.*

> *You don't feel like you are earning your own survival in the world, you feel like it's being handed to you. I grew up in an affluent suburb and I never had a sense as a young man that I was contributing in any way to the fact that I was physically alive on the planet...that kind of life is correlated with depression.*

> *The one thing that I cannot survive is that kind of complacent affluence...look at their suicide rates, their addiction rates, their depression rates.*

Benjamin Franklin has an answer for you, if you are looking for importance, challenge, community, and purpose. In 1727, when he was just twenty-one-years-old, he started a small club that he called *Junto*. He had five other "ingenious"[30] members besides himself, and although he was the youngest, he was their leader. They met once a week on Fridays for the purpose of "mutual improvement," and required members to "produce one or more queries on any point of Morals, Politics, or Natural Philosophy, to be discuss'd by the company; and once in three months produce and read an essay of his own writing, on any subject he pleased." They would debate differences civilly "in the sincere spirit of inquiry after truth, without fondness for dispute, or desire of victory" and eventually even banned "all expressions of positiveness in opinions, or direct contradiction."

I suggest you form your group in the spirit of the *Junto*. You should select who you invite to join your group carefully – it will be the most important decision you make in forming the *Junto*. The old adage *you are who your friends are* is true; what they do and who they are will eventually be what you do and who you are. Consider Franklin, who was the leader of his little group, but who was the youngest and presumably least experienced. He surrounded himself with people who would raise him up, not drag him down. Don't limit your invitations to people your own age who are from your school, but don't rule them out, either. They can be any age and from any place, so long as they are willing to meet, have an open mind, and are "ingenious." Again, *please* don't invite your friends simply because they are your friends. You are forming a group whose purpose is "mutual improvement" and public service, not video games and homework help.

Benjamin Franklin met with his *Junto* every Friday. I would suggest you try to meet once a week, or at least once every other week. Anything less than that and you won't be able to build a culture. The meeting should probably run between one and three hours, depending on how often you meet and what you hope to accomplish. Besides the writing and speaking requirements outlined above, members of the *Junto* could possibly consider these questions:[31]

---

[30] All quotes are from *Autobiography*

1. Have you read, watched, or listened to anything of value that you'd like to share?
2. Has anyone been rejected or failed at anything recently? What was the cause?
3. Has anyone succeeded in anything lately? What was the cause?
4. Have you heard about, or met, anybody who is rich? How did they become rich?
5. Is there anyone you have heard about who deserves praise? What did they attempt?
6. Have you or anyone you know lost your self-control in any area of life? What happened?
7. Have you or anyone you know gotten sick or hurt? What treatments did you try, and were they effective?
8. Have you gone on any trips? Are you planning trips? Do you know of anyone going on trips?
9. How might the *Junto* help this community?
10. Is there any young person who is ambitious in some endeavor, whom this *Junto* could help??
11. Has anyone, in the school, community, or elsewhere, had their rights violated? What can the *Junto* do to help?
12. Is there any successful or helpful person whom you would like to meet?
13. Have you stood up for anybody lately – bullies, gossip, etc.?
14. How can this *Junto* help you in your good deeds?
15. Is there anything you are struggling with in your life right now that the *Junto* may help with?
16. Has anyone helped you who is not here, and what can we do to thank them?
17. Is there a project that you wish to complete, and would like the *Junto's* help?
18. Are there any problems with the *Junto* that we can

---

[31] Copied and revised from *Autobiography*

address now?

Your *Junto* should have a structure and clearly defined agenda. It should allow for plenty of opportunities for everybody to participate, and for everybody's ideas and suggestions, but if you don't have a structure or an agenda, then you aren't going to accomplish what you wish to accomplish. You should also have rules for attendance, participation, and behavior. If these things aren't written and agreed upon, then it will be awkward if one person is counter to the culture you are trying to build, but hasn't done anything so egregious to be outright expelled. Structure, agenda, and expectations shouldn't be so draconian that people are dismissed for missing a meeting or being underprepared, but should be strict enough where people treat this as a fun way to better everyone in the group as well as the community as a whole. Again, the whole idea is *self-improvement* and *service to the community*.

Certain negative qualities of character should be instant indicators that the person is not right for the club, e.g., gossiping, laziness, bullying, etc. Someone who gossips about others to the club *will* gossip about the club to others, and that will destroy the spirit and culture of the *Junto*. There's nothing wrong with discussing someone's flopped attempt at public speaking if the spirit of the discussion is learning from someone's mistakes – and how wonderful if the club could improve their own skills, and possibly even help the person who flopped in future endeavors!

Forming a *Junto* is a good first, proactive, positive step towards seizing your education. You are making a statement – that you are responsible for your education and will control the trajectory of your self-betterment – while at the same time developing a culture that values knowledge, wisdom, and experience over filling yourself with someone else's data. It is a support unit as well as a team that will form the foundation for future endeavors in self-direction, as opposed to sitting around allowing yourself to be schooled. Don't treat this as an "extracurricular" or as some temporary fixture that exists to boost your resume. This *is* the curriculum, and where you go in your self-development, and what you accomplish in the community, is completely and totally up to you and the *Junto*.

You are the most important variable in the learning process. There is only one person in this universe that you must live and die with, and that's you. School isn't necessary for success, or the only way to reach your goals. It may be the best way to do certain things at certain times, but it certainly shouldn't control your life. Fire, water, motor vehicles, and school, are all valuable things when you control them, and deadly things when you cannot. You control your life, and *Junto* is a platform   to   help   you   make   that   happen.

11

PUBLISH AN UNDERGROUND NEWSLETTER

Daryl Davis is a Black musician who, since the 1980s, has been convincing members of the Ku Klux Klan to quit the group as well as their hateful beliefs.[32] He does what the Civil War, Jim Crow, and *Brown v. Board of Education* could not. The Civil War guaranteed the slaves freedom, but could not force the races to get along. The war not only left racism intact, it also left hundreds of thousands dead and added resentment along racial and regional lines. Jim Crow – physically separating the races "for their own good" – somehow didn't have the effect of bringing us all together. *Brown v. Board of Education* forced us into physical proximity, but you can't force understanding or love. What Davis has done that is mightier than any of these government interventions is this: he asks Klan members, "How can you

---

[32] *Black Man Gets KKK Members to Disavow by Befriending Them*
http://www.huffingtonpost.com/entry/black-man-daryl-davis-befriends-kkk-documentary-accidental-courtesy_us_585c250de4b0de3a08f495fc

hate me if you don't even know me?" Then he listens; this technique has resulted in the complete dissolution of the Klan in Maryland.

This isn't voodoo. Those of you who went to Sunday School know that Jesus walked with prostitutes and cursed tax collectors. If Jesus came back today, he'd probably eschew the Civil War, Jim Crow, and *Brown v. Board of Education* in favor of sitting down and talking with the people who hate us – because, simply, you can't bring about love by using violence.

Our freedom of speech is not some cute, optional, anachronistic thing that you write about on a short answer quiz about school uniforms or some such silliness. Your freedom to assemble (e.g., *Junto*), to create and distribute content, and to express yourself (e.g., to ask a Klan member *Why do you hate me when you don't know me?*), and to be able to do so without fear of violence or censorship (which are essentially the same thing), is absolutely fundamental to a free and just society. It is not a right *given* to you by the first Amendment – the first Amendment simply states what your human rights are. Even if the first were removed, even if it were amended, even if it were made illegal to voice certain opinions, your right for individual expression would still be as much a right as breathing. On this issue, rules and laws are irrelevant.

Are there exceptions? Speech that could reasonably infringe on the rights of others to life and freedom, the classic example of yelling *fire* in a movie theater. Plagiarism is obviously theft. These are common sense examples. Here's another concept: claiming *freedom of speech!* as an excuse to be a nasty person does not protect you from the consequences of what you say. Contrary to belief, you have both the constitutional and the human right to be a racist, sexist, bullying narcissist, or to curse like a sailor; nobody has the right to legislate you into good behavior. This does not mean you have the constitutional or human right to have friends, maintain employment, or to not be removed from someone else's property. If a college has a guest speaker, and they are speaking, you don't get to act like a fool and then claim a free speech violation when security comes to remove you. Similarly, you don't have the constitutional right to be invited to a college as a guest speaker, any more than you have a constitutional right to be invited to my living room.

On the other hand, if you choose to *never* be offensive, you are choosing to leave unengaged the "motor for human progress."[33] How offensive was it for Daryl Davis to walk into Grand Dragon Roger Kelly's house? Davis obviously offended Klan members, as well as members of the Black community who considered his fraternization a betrayal. Davis walked into the house of a man who would prefer see his race exterminated. Any kind of human or natural right that we have in this country has been a result of some person offending some group. Of course, you could also stand on the street corner and scream insults at anyone who walks by, or preach that people *can say these words* and *can't say these words*, and claim that you are a warrior for social change.

How do you know the difference between being offensive for the good of society, and simply being a jerk? The same way the young and foolish have become old and wise throughout all of human history: listening to varying viewpoints, testing them through experience, and arriving through a series of successes and failures to a personal code of conduct. Students need the time and space to engage with a range of perspectives and to make mistakes.

Sticks and stones will break my bones but words will never hurt me is just silly. Don Miguel Ruiz argues in his book *The Four Agreements* that the first agreement you should have with yourself is to be "impeccable," or perfect, with your words. Why does the idea of a witch's spell make sense to us? What is a prayer or a curse? How can we enchant objects such as flags or crucifixes or wedding rings or war medals or currency

---

[33] *Freedom of Speech and Right to Offend* Brendan O'Neill
https://youtu.be/BtWrljX9HRA

and transform them into more than their physical composition? There is a relationship between our words and our thoughts, our words and the words that we hear or read, our words and our beliefs, and our words and our actions. We can cast spells and have spells cast on us. Our freedom of speech isn't important because words are impotent; our freedom of speech is important *because* our words are powerful.

To have a society that is free and just, individuals must have the opportunity to contribute to the marketplace of ideas. Make it part of your personal code of conduct to defend the free-flowing market of ideas at all costs, however controversial or vile those ideas, and to allow those ideas to stand or fall on their merits. It has become fashionable to ban speakers from colleges for having what is perceived as distasteful ideas – why? If Daryl Davis can sit down and have a fireside chat with men whose parents and grandparents considered lynching a reasonable strategy in dealing with the darky, then I think undergraduates should be able to handle a frank discussion on how many genders need their own bathroom.

Middle and high school relies heavily on an appeal to authority. In other words, teachers, school administrators, the board of education, and the state, all have a monopoly on the transmission of ideas. They hold "truth" on the basis of their authority instead of allowing truth, or at least the dialectic process of approaching truth, to be the authority. They decide which subjects are required, which topics are taught within those subjects, how they are assessed, and how, if at all, students may contribute. Generally speaking, ideas or questions that are too provocative or offensive are avoided, unless the provocation fits the school's view of itself. Also, expect a fight against anything that challenges the power of a teacher, administrator, etc. From kindergarten until senior year, there is virtually no opportunity for students to criticize, debate, affirm, or otherwise dialogue between themselves, the school, their family, or the community, on *anything* that happens at school, from social events to curriculum to staffing to clubs. Students exercise the first amendment by answering questions that the teachers ask and chatting with their peers at lunch. For the few who are involved in the school paper, that is censored by the adult club advisor under the guidance of the school district. That is the extent of the practice students will get with the free-flowing market of ideas.

There is a way for students who decide to stay in school to take back their first amendment rights by publishing an "underground" school newspaper,[34] but a few cautions must be taken. Personally, I'm not against breaking laws or rules if it means reclaiming individual freedom, but it is also not helpful to leap without looking. Here are how students can take control without running afoul of Johnny Law:

1. As I mentioned earlier, no school resources may be used, to include school computers, school printers, and school staff. This is unfortunate, but true. It would certainly be helpful to have some adults help, whether it's by contributing money for printing or insight into the kind of stories to run, but if anyone from the school helps, it becomes a *de facto* school activity, and thus can be censored.

2. Students may not disrupt the normal operation of the school. You cannot interrupt class to distribute newsletters, stage or suggest protests such as walk-outs or blocking the hallways, or interrupt any other staff in their daily duties. You may distribute newsletters before and after school, during lunch shifts, during study halls, or in between classes.

3. All the normal and hopefully common sense rules for journalism apply: you may not plagiarize, be

---

[34] *Do First Amendment Rights Apply to Students in School?* By Peter Gray https://www.psychologytoday.com/blog/freedom-learn/201508/do-first-amendment-rights-apply-students-in-school

pornographic, threaten, incite violence, slander (*slander* is different from *criticize* – the former is untrue and damaging to an individual), and so on. Use the power of speech to offend, as is your right, but attempting to garner vapid attention in foolish ways should be left to the professional news media; you are fighting for something much larger and much more important than that.

It may be just as easy, or easier, to publish on social media than print. There are pros and cons to print and digital, and there isn't anything to prevent you from doing both except time and money. Those are the details that I will leave to you, dear reader. I would suggest an anonymous e-mail, such as AnonHS@email.com, where people can send suggestions for stories. If you're old fashioned you could also set up a PO Box, but besides that, I'll leave distribution to you all.

What *does* belong in an underground newsletter? Anything you want! You probably don't want to limit yourself to the kinds of stuff that would be found in a school sanctioned newspaper. If that's what you're interested in, then join the school paper and utilize all the resources the school has to offer. Your underground newsletter should make it a point to stimulate real dialogue. Consider some of the things you talk about in your *Junto* – in fact, an underground newsletter may be one of the missions of *Junto* – but make sure you work out anonymity and that the fellow members are comfortable with sharing. The last thing you want is to undermine the trust of the group. You could interview school staff, students, or community members, and use their insight on some aspect of school. You may think, as I do, that students need experience more than they need algebra.[35] Why not pose that as a question, and write a piece on how school could make that a

---

[35] *We Need Experience More Than We Need Algebra* by John Taylor Gatto http://www.lifelearningmagazine.com/1212/we-need-experience-more-than-we-need-algebra.htm

reality for students. Attend board meetings – depending on your district, a lot goes on at these things. Make the anonymous e-mail or PO Box available to everybody for leads, and be certain you keep any lead anonymous. In New York, you can do a FOIL request for any school employee's e-mails, and there is similar legislation in other states. In other words, you can request e-mails to or from any teacher, administrator, or anyone with a district e-mail, and the state must provide them to you. I'm not an advocate for needlessly harassing school district employees, or singling people out for no reason, but on the other hand, these are the people who are supposed to be serving you. It's fair to keep them honest. There is enough going on at any given school to have weekly blog posts on social media, and monthly print newsletters.

Some school-people will commend what you are doing, but many, probably even good ones, will resist the idea that an underground newsletter, that is, a relatively untethered opportunity for student free speech, as something of value. They'll probably see it as outright defiance, or possibly well-intentioned but misguided. This is because most of us have internalized the unwritten rules of school: you are an employee at a low-skill job, and the grownups are your boss. You are to comply because we don't want a cheeseburger-by-committee. Ketchup, mustard, onions, pickle, pass; ketchup, mustard, onions, pickle, pass. That is not what an education is. Stay the course, don't quit, and, just like the *Junto*, recruit good people from the underclassman as you move up the grades. Your underground newsletter will be an interesting oddity that lasts a year or two if you don't expose the next round of kids to the culture of what you're doing and what you hope to accomplish.

Depending on your district and what you choose to post and print, it is probable that you wind up in the principal's office. They might collect and destroy your newsletters, punish you with detention or suspensions, and threaten to pull you off of teams and out of clubs. These are all violations of your rights – so long as you follow the guidelines in this chapter, you should be aboveboard legally (remember to check with your state). It won't stop them from doing it. Any beast that's cornered lashes out. This is where it is important to have your parents' support. Don't lose your temper or your dignity, believe in the purity of what you are doing, and stay the course. Do not take down your site. Do not stop printing your newsletter. Mobilize the community. A school administrator is not authorized to block or destroy an independent newsletter. Do not give in to bullies. With love in your heart, *fight*.

Asserting your freedom of press at school is not simply rabblerousing, or for venting over homework. I love rabblerousing and I hate homework, but if that was all you were doing, then you might as well just rant on your own social media. You are making the statement that you, individually and collectively as a student body, are there; you are important; you have control over how this whole *school* thing is going to go; you will be heard. It's good and just that you practice on teachers and school principals, because one day you are going to have to live in a world of lawmakers and tax collectors, and you should have some sense of how to use your freedom of speech to claim control over your life.

12

STAY DEBT FREE

Soon you are going to get it put into your head that you ought to go to college. And you probably should. However, you are fast approaching one of the most dangerous moments of your life, the sort that could impact the kind of stability you are going to have in your personal and professional life for the next twenty-five years.

In my experience, the questions students ask about college and financial aid are usually geared around how to fill out the online forms for college loans. It's shocking there aren't more programs warning students of how a couple of clicks on a FAFSA could alter the trajectory of their life forever. The government *will* loan you a hundred thousand dollars, if that's how much your school costs. At which point, you *must* pay the money back, usually over the course of either ten or twenty-five years. You cannot discharge these loans in bankruptcy like you could with credit cards and personal loans. You cannot sell your degree like you could sell a house or a car. A forty thousand dollar car is probably a poor choice, but if you sell it for thirty thousand then all that means is you made a ten thousand dollar mistake, not a forty thousand dollar mistake. A hundred thousand dollar student loan mistake is a hundred thousand dollar student loan mistake. You discharge student loans through complete payment, permanent disability, or death. One other option is to flee the country,[36] although technically that doesn't discharge the loans. Those are your only options.

Student loans stick around even if you fail to finish your degree program. If you finish 117 credits of a 120 credit BA, you don't get 97.5% of a degree. You get nothing but loans. A significant number of students withdraw from college without completing their degree program. If your private college is forty thousand dollars a year and after year one you decide college isn't for you, you have forty thousand dollars' worth of loans to pay off and nothing to show for it.

Let's round up and say that the average recent graduate makes fifty thousand dollars a year. You might make more, you'll probably make less, and you might not get a job at all, but for the purpose of this urgent math lesson, let's say you're a twenty-year-old graduate making fifty thousand dollars a year, or about $2,770 a month after government theft.

---

[36] Countries without extradition treaties with the United States according to Wikipedia: Afghanistan, Algeria, Andorra, Angola, Armenia, Bahrain, Bangladesh, Belarus, Botswana, Brunei, Burkina Faso, Burma, Burundi, Cambodia, Cameroon, Cape Verde, Central African Republic, Chad, China (except Hong Kong), Comoros, Congo (Kinshasa), Djibouti, Equatorial Guinea, Eritrea, Ethiopia, Gabon, Guinea, Guinea-Bissau, Indonesia, Ivory Coast, Kazakhstan, Kuwait, Laos, Lebanon, Libya, Madagascar, Maldives, Mali, Marshall Islands, Mauritania, Mexico, Micronesia, Moldova, Mongolia, Morocco, Mozambique, Namibia, Nepal, Niger, North Korea, Oman, Qatar, Russia, Rwanda, Samoa, São Tomé & Príncipe, Saudi Arabia, Senegal, Somalia, Sudan, South Sudan, Syria, Togo, Tunisia, Uganda, Ukraine, United Arab Emirates, Uzbekistan, Vanuatu, Vatican City, Vietnam, Yemen.

School[37] and Residency Status	Loan balance	Monthly payment	Years to Pay Off
State School On Campus	$80,520	**$854**	10
State School On Campus	$80,520	**$471**	25
State School Commuter	$47,360	**$502**	10
State School Commuter	$47,360	**$277**	25
Private School On Campus	$181,412	**$1,924**	10
Private School On Campus	$181,412	**$1,061**	25
Private School Commuter	$129,172	**$1,370**	10
Private School Commuter	$129,172	**$755**	25

If you lived on campus at your private school, and you

---

[37] Actual numbers based on Colleges in the Albany, New York area, as of 2016.

were fortunate enough to graduate and land a job right away at fifty thousand dollars a year, then you're looking at a monthly payment that is practically your entire monthly paycheck up until your early thirties. Or maybe you lived on campus at a state school, and now you're paying $471 every month until you're nearly fifty-years-old. Maybe some birdie whispered in your ear that the way to double your income is to go to graduate school, so you put your loans in deferment, took out another thirty thousand dollars in loans, and now you're paying both loans, except you never actually increased your income.

Let me tell you how it feels to know you are going to be paying between 20% and 70% or even 100% of your income to student loans for the next 25 years. It feels like you're a senior in high school, it's June, and the principal calls you in the office to tell you the state has changed the regulations, and you have six more years of high school before you can graduate. It's your coach telling you that you have two more sprints, then telling you that those sprints weren't good enough so you have twenty more. It's going on a fifteen-mile hike in the most rugged of rugged mountains, having it rain, having it sleet, having it be a fourteen-hour death-march knowing that it's a six-hour drive home, and getting to your car only to realize you left the keys with your pack at the top of the mountain and you have no other choice but to go back and get them. It's devastating. It's soul-crushing. It's demoralizing. And while mathematically you could take a second or third job and work through the debt in less than five years, you probably won't, because you'll be so emotionally drained by the sheer enormity of the numbers. Helpless, hopeless, and out of control. You'll have no personal freedom, and be in a position where even the most enlightened yogi would find it difficult to fill their heart with love.

You have no idea how hard it will be to sleep until you see how little you make compared to how much you have to pay. It will impact your professional and personal life, delay things like buying a house or having kids, and limit your ability to save for retirement. Your romantic relationships will be strained; if you have a thousand dollars a month in student loans, for a period of ten to twenty-five years, then how could they not be?

There's another side of the equation we haven't touched yet. Theoretically, every dollar you're paying out to student loans could have been invested in a retirement account. You could be losing *literally millions of dollars*. Take the exact same monthly payments, for the exact same amount of time, and instead of handing it over to the feds, see what happens when you invest it:[38]

Monthly contribution to retirement plan	Years contributions are made, beginning at age 22	Approximate amount, retirement, age 65
$854	10	$1.9m
$471	25	$1.7m
$502	10	$1.1m
$277	25	$971k
$1,924	10	$4.2m
$1,061	25	$3.7m
$1,370	10	$3m
$755	25	$2.6m

Of course, if you were investing *x* amount for ten years, it probably makes sense you'd continue until retirement. Most people don't just invest for ten years and then call it quits. Continue the forty-three years until retirement and you're looking at a range of between $1.1 million and $7.6 million.

If a principal suggested eliminating sex education from the curriculum, they'd wind up on the front page, and yet individuals can wait indefinitely to have sex – nobody can wait indefinitely before they have to deal with money. If I

---

[38] At 8%, retiring at sixty-five-years-old.

were to teach the money-version of sex-ed, this is what I'd teach:

1) Your major matters more than your school in terms of Return On Investment. A BA in Underwater Fire Prevention from Yale is less useful than a Business Administration degree from State U. Just because a degree doesn't have a great ROI doesn't mean it's worthless – philosophy and poetry, for example, are both intrinsically valuable. However, there *is* some math to consider. Is the degree intrinsically valuable to the tune of $800 a month for a decade?

2) Let me reiterate a point: *the world needs more philosophers and poets.* I'm not patronizing – I couldn't be more serious. We need more of those sorts of people in education, business, law, politics, now more than ever. This is especially true, ironically, of the military. Separating the philosopher and poet from the soldier creates one group of deep-thinking cowards and another group of non-thinking killers. However, there is a mathematical reality to confront (hopefully by your freshman or sophomore year of high school). Be the best you that you can be throughout high school,[39] win as many grants and scholarships as you can, and limit or preferably eliminate the necessity of mortgaging your life for your humanities degree. The chapters in Part Two of this book are meant to be an outline for how you might realize your greatest potential.

3) "Self-betterment," e.g., resume building for no other sake than scholarship money or college admissions, has the same reek of the grades-as-an-economic-transaction philosophy. However, scholarship money is out there, and the type of people who get the money are the type of people who have spent years developing themselves

---

[39] See *Confessions of a Scholarship Winner: The Secrets That Helped Me Win $500,000 in Free Money for College* by Kristina Ellis

into the best version of themselves they can be. Jim Hightower said *Even a dead fish can go with the flow.* We're looking for well-muscled salmon.

4) If you or your family is rich and they are going to pay your tuition, or if you have a college fund that will cover the tuition of an expensive school, or it's covered through scholarships, and you want to go, then go. Everybody else: get your degree as cheaply as possible. This isn't just about saving money; it's about minimizing risk and maximizing freedom. You have no idea if you'll get a job upon graduation and you have no idea how much it'll pay if you do get one. Degrees that were marketable when you began your program may suddenly not be. Also, you may find you want to backpack Europe while you're still young, or open a business outside of what your major was. You don't have the freedom to do these things if you are on the hook for hundreds or thousands of dollars in payments every month for the next half of your life.

5) The process itself is your education, the degree is your credential. Figuring out how to pay for college,[40] then rolling up your sleeves and working through school while managing classes, rent, food, and other bills, *is* where you get your education. It's where you become an adult. The paper in the frame is what you show your prospective employer, but what you did to get it free and clear of debt is your actual education.

Of course, this is all assuming you should go to college at all. If I had a nickel for every student who said, "I'm going to college but I don't know why," I'd be rich. Why sentence yourself to four more years of school two months after surviving thirteen years of school? Why not at least consider

---

[40] "COULD I live in a van?"
http://www.nytimes.com/2013/04/14/education/edlife/ken-ilgunas-lives-in-a-van-while-a-graduate-student-at-duke-university.html

taking some time off before going? Malia Obama decided to take a gap year. Why the visceral reaction towards exploring options? Most millionaires in America own their own business – why not consider an internship or apprenticeship? Myriads of successful people come from the military or the Peace Corps, and jobs you get through trade school can never be outsourced to Asia.[41]

There are two obvious reasons to go to college. The first reason is for the credential, e.g., certification (teachers, doctors, lawyers, nurses, accountants, etc.). The second, as a means of self-exploration or the exploration of an interest in which you'd want to surround yourself with like-minded people. Both of those things can be valuable. The "college experience" is fantastic for some people, but if that *experience* from your perspective is primarily parties, then as your unofficial financial consultant, I'd like to advise you that there is a much cheaper way to experience keg stands and bong hits than forty thousand dollars a year. Whatever the reason you're going, make sure you have one, and make sure it doesn't leave you a twenty-two-year-old slave. School should serve you, not the other way around.

Not getting a college degree has been stigmatized – everybody can at least get into community college. The story goes that if you're not going, that means there is something wrong with you. It is the expressed mission of many high schools to prepare you for college, no matter what. This is a handy piece of sociology to know when it comes time to jack up tuition.

If a friend or family member asks you to cosign a loan, that means the bank has determined that there is a statistical likelihood of that person being unable to make the monthly payments. It is a bank's job to predict if someone is capable of paying back a certain amount of money, and banks are

---

[41] If working outside or with your hands appeals to you, I'd encourage you to listen to and read Mike Rowe;
http://profoundlydisconnected.com/foundation/

very good at making that prediction. The federal government "cosigns" your student loans. Actually, they own your loans, because no bank would hand over thirty thousand dollars a year to an eighteen-year-old in hopes they might actually complete a degree, get a job, and pay back a hundred and twenty thousand dollars, with interest. It's a huge risk for the banks, but the federal government can just go into your paycheck, your bank account, or deploy steroid-abusing storm troopers to raid your home. So they don't mind handing out college money. That's why there is more college loan debt than credit card debt in America.

Ask yourself this: if a private lender were approached by an eighteen-year-old with no job, no assets, no references besides maybe a guidance counselor and a geometry teacher, and they had a *good* idea for an investment, do you think that lender would hand $80k to that kid? Not a chance. So why would the government hand over that same amount for a degree that has zero value in the marketplace? Because institutions like governments that don't produce anything require dependency from citizenry. A government's existence requires your dependency, although the dirty little secret is that no Democrat or Republican is coming to save you. If you were independent, you'd need them less. Government-owned loans are also the disincentive for colleges to price tuition reasonably. The loans are guaranteed, the kids are lined up to come, so why not charge as much as you'd like?

You could think in a groove and live your life on a train, letting the tracks take you wherever the tracks take you. Or you could be intentional and informed about your decisions, and have a plan for your life. There are very few jobs that justify fifty or sixty thousand dollars a year for four years in order to be "qualified." Be creative and be informed. Transfer community college credits. Take *CLEP* exams.[42] Get a four-year degree in six years and pay cash by working a full-time job. Or a full-time job and a part-time job. Know what you're

---

[42] https://clep.collegeboard.org/exams

working toward and eliminate debt, so that if you change your mind later it doesn't kill you to know you have a hundred thousand dollar biology degree hanging in the kitchen of the tapas restaurant you just opened.

13

SELF-RELIANCE

Jia Jiang wanted to become the next Bill Gates.[43] The problem was, he was paralyzed by the thought of rejection. Luckily, he was self-aware enough to know this about himself, and decided to be proactive. He sat down and sketched out a hundred ridiculous things he could ask strangers in an attempt to purposely get rejected a hundred times. He set out to do one a day – things like *ask a stranger to borrow a hundred dollars* and *knock on someone's door and ask to plant a flower in their backyard* – and to record his exploits and publish them online in a video blog.

Jiang was successful: he built self-confidence by confronting his fear of rejection. But some other strange thing happened with Jiang's little social experiment. He wasn't always rejected – in fact, with his viral video requesting "Olympic Donuts" from a Krispy Kreme employee, the employee set to work with energy and pride[44] (recall the

---

[43] *What I learned from a hundred days of rejection*, Jia Jiang
https://www.youtube.com/watch?v=-vZXgApsPCQ

conditions that lead to job satisfaction: come to work willingly; know the purpose of the work; be able to express yourself in your work. Watch Jackie work and tell me she doesn't find happiness in those conditions being met). Jiang also found that he could sometimes turn a rejection into an opportunity by asking *why not* and entering into negotiations. For example, by asking why the stranger wouldn't let him plant a flower in his backyard, the man said he had a flower-hating dog, and referred him to a lady across the street, who gladly accepted his offer to plant a flower.

In 2014 I started a college scholarship endowment for refugee students who were graduates of Albany High School, where I taught. I had a goal of reaching $25,000 in a year and a half. I had no idea if that was a lot or a little. I had never attempted anything like this. I met with a representative from the local state university who would manage the endowment, I set up a website, and I signed up for a Facebook account for the first time. I took time off from work and visited dozens of business with fliers. I e-mailed and called media outlets. At a certain point, looking at the endowment balance, I was disheartened to think that I would have been better off getting a part time job at minimum wage, and would have raised more money and worked less hours.

I believe it was NPR who contacted me first, and I did an eight-minute interview on the radio. Then some local TV stations interviewed both myself and some refugee students. Staff members, including our communications specialist, as well as a student who made a promotional video, volunteered to help, and now "I'm raising money" turned into "we're raising money." A few blogs picked it up. We were on the front page of the local paper. We were on Fox National News.[45] Friends, family, coworkers, and complete strangers were giving hundreds, sometimes thousands, of dollars. Even after reaching our goal, another teacher picked up the mantle

---

[44] https://www.youtube.com/watch?v=7Ax2CsVbrX0
[45] http://brianhuskie.com/interviews-and-articles/

and, completely on her own, designed and sold T-shirts for the endowment, raising over a thousand dollars in just a few weeks.

It wasn't easy, and in the spirit of Jiang's experiment, I was rejected a lot. Not only was I rejected, at first, by media and by businesses, I also had to make myself vulnerable in front of, essentially, the world. More to the point, I put myself in an awkward space in front of *my* world: I cried in front of students and I cried in front of the Fox news crew, with a former student present. I cried in front of my wife half a dozen times, and I cried while writing essays meant to persuade people to donate. I cried more in those two years than I had cried from age five to thirty-four. For an infantryman who is supposed to be able to eat lead and shit bullets, that's embarrassing. As I attempted to convey in the first half of this book, it's been an emotional ride: Iraq and everything that happened in 2004, teaching Iraqi kids, having kids of my own, standing by helpless as more and more refugees are created in large part by our own government, and working in a profession that thinks testing refugee students for eighteen hours straight is a measured and reasonable way to assess "twenty-first century skills." It's all what inspired me to start the endowment. It's what inspired me to write this book. Like all things worth talking and learning about, it's emotional.

Efficacy – your ability to produce a desired result – is closely tied to self-confidence. They are practically synonyms. Self-confidence has nothing to do with everybody getting a trophy. It has nothing to do with winning at everything you do. It has to do with knowing in your heart that you can succeed, despite failures, and if success is impossible in *this*, then it's time to move on to *that*. You can turn failure into success. You can learn. Just as you can't be grateful and hateful at the same time, you can't be confident and fearful at the same time. I don't mean startled or nervous – fearful is full of fear. It's a more permanent state of being. Have faith in yourself and your abilities. You are willing to take risks, to fail, to be vulnerable, to try again and again. You take initiative; you act. The Universe favors movement over stagnation, or as I was told growing up, God helps those who help themselves. You are emotionally invested; you have passion and love.

Self-reliance means you trust yourself. It means that you don't *rely* on other people's work, or other people's assessment. Reliance on others is dependency, and dependency is for children. People often counter this with *you live in a society* or *you have to learn to collaborate* or *you don't live on an island in the eighteenth century.* All of those things are true – it is also true that if you aren't any use to yourself, then you aren't going to be any use collaborating in this great societal collective that everyone keeps telling me I belong to. Every great athlete playing on a team has to bring himself or herself to the gym, and they have to put their own two hands on the barbell, and they have to lift. Every master carpenter in every construction company has to drive each nail into each two-by-four with his or her own two hands. Jiang had to have the heart to approach strangers and be rejected before he could start his own company whose mission is to help others with rejection. I had to decide that I was willing to make myself emotionally vulnerable, as well as possibly fail in reaching my goal of $25,000, before I could collaborate with anyone else. If you aren't self-reliant – if you can't rely on yourself – then which group in their right mind would want to rely on you?

Developing self-reliance in school is challenging, because the system is built on dependency on evaluations from authority in the form of grades, punishment for failure in the form of grades and high-stakes tests, and an indifference to individual passions. It produces students who are neurotic, who either convince themselves that a teacher's arbitrary numeric valuation of students is valid and reliable, in which case students learn to do just about anything without question to earn that extrinsic reward, which also serves as an affirmation of the student's superiority over their peers (or, if they score too low, it is a devastating indictment on their self-worth), or, they internalized years of mediocre grades and come to believe they are a mediocre person, who then do just enough to pass, but view grades as an economic transaction rather than an opportunity for self-betterment, e.g., *doing these things gets me enough points to be released from this place.*

The first step to claiming self-reliance in a school setting is to not take grades very seriously. Make your own decisions for your own life, and reject this fake economy that exists merely to control your behavior and has the secondary effect of undermining your love of learning. Of course, taking this attitude will make it impossible for school-people to, as they are wont to say, *hold you accountable,* and it is possible, depending on how far you take this, that they will try to force you into an alternative placement, or reject you from the system entirely. Be clear on your own goals. If you plan on being accepted to a competitive college, and you insist on remaining in a school setting, then grades are going to be important. However, don't conflate your grades with your self-efficacy, self-esteem, or knowledge; everyone knows that you forget what's taught after the test is given.[46] Grades are, at their core, someone else's idea of how you performed at some arbitrary set of tasks and behaviors, usually while sitting motionless for hours at a time. They are a measure of your compliance; they are a valuation of how much of a dependent you are. Erica Goldson said in her 2010 Valedictory speech, *I have successfully shown that I was the best slave. I did what I was told to the extreme.*[47] If you want an education, then you have to seize it yourself; you need to practice self-reliance.

What are some practical things that you can do to build your self-reliance? Read about people who have done the same — are there any successful people who had a smooth

---

[46] *Summer Slide? There's No Such Thing* by Kerry McDonald
http://www.wbur.org/cognoscenti/2017/06/28/rethinking-education-unschooling-kerry-mcdonald
[47] *Here I Stand* by Erica Goldson
http://americaviaerica.blogspot.com/2010/07/coxsackie-athens-valedictorian-speech.html

road to success? People would have you believe that all millionaires were sons and daughters of millionaires, but the book *The Millionaire Next Door* by Thomas Stanley and William Danko claims that about 80% of all millionaires are first-generation wealthy. You have to consider, also, that even those who inherit great wealth need to be able to keep it. It's a lot easier to spend money than to save or make it. Anyone, who has had great success in anything, not just with money, has had to rely on themselves, and has had to experience failure. Be inspired by these people.

Of course, in order to practice building self-reliance, you have to actually do something. Starting the *Junto*, or an underground newsletter, or taking control of your own finances and paying for college without accumulating debt, are all great suggestions. Learn how to use tools and build or maintain things: a doghouse, a dollhouse, change the oil in the car, change the blinds in the house, drive a nail, measure and cut a board, etc. Learn how to survive a few nights in the woods. Learn firearm safety and learn how to shoot. Design and build a garden, as simple or as elaborate as you'd like. Do not underestimate the value of nutrition and physical fitness; your body, mind, and soul are all connected. If you poison one of those things, then you poison them all. Your ability to produce food, e.g., gardening, hunting, and fishing, and your physical fitness, are the cornerstones of true self-reliance upon which everything else is built. Of course, you should probably begin by cleaning your room. Robert Heinlein in his science fiction novel *Time Enough for Love* gives a pretty good summary of the type of person I'm describing:

> *A human being should be able to change a diaper, plan an invasion, butcher a hog, conn a ship, design a building, write a sonnet, balance accounts, build a wall, set a bone, comfort the dying, take orders, give orders, cooperate, act alone, solve equations, analyze a new problem, pitch manure, program a computer, cook a tasty meal, fight efficiently, die gallantly. Specialization is for insects.*

Don't ever be the victim, even when – especially when – you've been victimized. Self-reliant people don't do that. Strong, confident people don't blame other people or situations for their failures. Even if you're on a party-cruise in the Bahamas, and your ship sinks, and a hurricane is coming in. Are you going to splash around and weep and curse that stupid captain or that dumb reef or the goddamn low-pressure system or those useless women and children who boarded the life boats before you? Are you a victim of your circumstances who can do nothing to survive? Bullshit! Kick! Swim! Scream! You're not dead yet! Lash two sharks together and ride them like a goddamn superhero! Playing the victim does nothing but sap your life force and make you dependent on other people or circumstances. Anyone who tries to convince you that you're a victim and that you should act accordingly is channeling the devil.

14

DROP OUT

There are as many ways to take an education as there are people on this earth. Actually, there are more ways to take an education as there are people, since our lives are videos and not snapshots, and the methods by which we "become educated" change over time. One thing is for certain – traditional school may be useful, or it may be harmful, but it's definitely not necessary. Withdrawing from school and completing your own independent program may be the most "radical" approach, when compared to societal norms, but it is also normal for a third of our society to be obese, half to be divorced, and eighty percent of us to be in debt. I don't spend much time with "normal."

There are a number of books and alternative schools that might help give you context beyond what I describe. Grace Llewelyn and Blake Boles wrote incredible guides, *The Teenage Liberation Handbook* and *College Without High School* (respectively); I also found *Homeschooling for Excellence* by David and Micki Colfax helpful. Look into the Sudbury School, the Albany Free School, North Star Learning Center, and other democratic schools, as well as the reading program developed by Nancie Atwell at the Center for Teaching and Learning in Maine. All of these resources demonstrate the power of freedom in claiming your education.

I'm going to offer you a possible program. It is not the only way to take an education, but you might find it helpful to have some kind of structure when considering the kind of experiences you want to have. First, as with all things, this will only be made possible with the blessing of your parents. I do not minimize the kind of courage this will take for everyone involved. Your family and friends are going to think you are crazy, they may think your parents are acting irresponsibly, and there may (or may not) be conflict with your home district. In order to make this work legally, you are going to have to register as *homeschooled*, which carries with it its own stigmas. You may be perceived as that kid who wears a colander as a hat and can't talk to peers without speaking in Klingon, or maybe you're that family who hates Darwin so much that your parents are willing to hide you in the basement until they've properly instructed the devil out of you. I encourage you to think of *homeschool* as the legal mechanism necessary to put yourself through your own "school." Make sure all the legalities are in order so as not to be distracted from the business of living your life.

Some people think it would be impossible, or more challenging, to get into college without a high school degree.[48] The short answer to that is, it depends. The slightly longer answer is, thousands of home-schooled kids, as well as foreign students whose academic credentials aren't from standard American or western schools, are admitted into colleges every year. Every school has its own admissions

---

[48] *Homeschool Applicants* by Matt McGann is specific to MIT, but offers some insight to homeschool applicants to college in general: http://mitadmissions.org/blogs/entry/homeschooled_applicants; As does *There's a New Path to Harvard and it's not in a Classroom* by Chris Weller: http://www.businessinsider.com/homeschooling-is-the-new-path-to-harvard-2015-9

requirements, and it's up to you to find out what that is and to do the things that get you into the schools you want to get into. Large research universities tend to be data driven, so without grades, you're going to have to rely more heavily on standardized tests such as the SATs, SAT subject tests, or CLEP exams, and possibly take some community college classes. This should be enough to demonstrate competency for university. Small private schools tend to be more holistic in their admissions policies, but also tend to be more expensive.

There are certainly "cons" to withdrawing from school, besides your family and friends thinking you're crazy (I actually think being thought of as "crazy" is a "pro"). Joining sports teams and things like the marching band become more challenging, depending on your state of residence. Ironically, the most useful parts of school are usually after school, such as sports and clubs and other things students consent to. You likely wouldn't have access to these things if you withdrew from school. You're on the hook financially for things like art supplies and science equipment. The onus is on you to actually accomplish something, rather than sit around and wait for someone else to tell you how to act, although I think this may be a "pro," too.

There are many benefits to getting away from traditional school. You get to control the direction of your life rather than allow yourself to be physically controlled by bells and to be conditioned like Pavlov's dog. You can learn the stuff that you'd learn in school, if you like (most of it isn't that hard), but also learn literally anything else you have a natural bend towards, instead of being force-fed area of a circle, how World War One started, and what anaphora means, only to forget it as soon as you take the test. You can learn to be at peace with yourself. You can complete personalized projects, and only take the standardized tests you choose to take. You can let your accomplishments speak for themselves, rather than wait on some expert's numeric valuation of your knowledge and skill. You can learn anywhere and anytime, surrounded by real people in the real world, rather than allow yourself to be cut off from the community, relegated to a single classroom on a closed campus. You can choose to value self-direction rather than compliance; it is the right path to take. It has been said, *Morality is doing what's right, no matter what you're told. Obedience is doing what you're told, no matter what's right.*

It takes about five thousand hours to complete high school, and during those hours you'll get virtually no responsibility. You'll get the responsibility of getting to class on time, with the consequence of having to spend more time in school in the form of detention. This is where they lecture you on how when you have a job, you have to get to the job on time. Because it takes the average teenager three or four thousand tries over four years to learn that a boss wants you to be on time. If you can't figure out that your boss wants you at work when your schedule says you should work, then you have much bigger problems. I'm convinced that born-again truants find their way to class on time for no other reason than they are sick of hearing the same idiotic lecture from the lifer with the tweed jacket who relishes teaching the youth about life. You'll also get the responsibility of doing the homework they assign you, dressing the way they tell you, speaking in ways they find appropriate, and keeping your cell phone, the single most powerful device the common man has ever had access to, away in your locker. All of this is a huge waste of your time, and completely unnecessary.

Do yourself a favor and survey a dozen or more non-educators over the age of thirty or forty. Ask them the top five things they remember from high school. Odds are they'll say something like prom, the big game, lunch with friends, the bus rides, a fight, breakups, cliques, drugs, a pain-in-the-ass teacher, an inspirational teacher, and just about anything but the actual "content" that eclipses everything else time-wise, good and bad, that happens in school. I'm not proud of this, but I had no idea you had to register and insure a car when I bought my first car around the age of twenty. Neither do most of the seniors I quiz on this little fun fact. They have no idea how to do their taxes, how much taxes are, how much college is, how to save for retirement, how to cook, how to fill out a check, how to make friends outside of school, how to approach a place of business for work, how to drive a stick shift, or how to get a credit card and why you shouldn't.

Nothing is treated with importance in high school. We generally don't teach those practical things like cooking and credit cards, but there is potential for importance in unpragmatic things such as how to determine the tone of a passage, factoring trinomials, how many subatomic particles are paired with their charges, and that George Washington called for policy neutrality in the 1790s. Nothing wrong with learning any of these things, but when they are forced and without context, then we are teaching you how to waste your time with inane, disconnected, arbitrary trivia. You would get more out of volunteering yourself as a serf on a farm in a foreign country for two weeks than four years of high school.[49]

What you'll get in school is shoved in a pod with a group of same-aged peers whom you may or may not know and like, with a stranger as a pod-leader demanding that you follow her script (really someone else's script that she is parroting) or face the consequences. Repeat for five thousand hours. It's mostly an unnecessary waste of your preciously short and rapidly dwindling life.

John Taylor Gatto's line from his book *Dumbing Us Down* might be a good rule of thumb when considering the design of your own education program:

> *Independent study, community service, adventures and experience, large doses of privacy and solitude, a thousand different apprenticeships — the one-day variety or longer —*

---

[49] I first read about the *World Wide Organization of Organic Farming* (http://wwoof.net/) in Blake Bole's book *College Without Highschool: A Teenager's Guide to Skipping High School and Going to College.*

these are all powerful, cheap, and effective ways to start a real reform of schooling.

I'm going to be specific about "program/graduation requirements," but keep in mind that even my program is pretty arbitrary. It's a good place to start, and may give some desired structure, but *personalized* means it's your own.[50]

Service to the Community

Volunteer work is essential for a young person to learn humility, self-less service, and to recognize they are of use in the world. It also connects them to the community and connects the community to them. Through community service they learn more about themselves, and more about the world around them. I would have a goal of seventy-two hours of community service per trimester (every three months).

Personal projects

Science fiction writers predict the future because they create worlds that straddle credulity.[51] They tend to be better fortunetellers than gypsies with crystal balls because they challenge scientists and inventors with what might be. Once you see or read something, even fiction, a spell has been cast. Running a mile in less than four minutes was thought to be dangerous to attempt and impossible for a human to accomplish, until it was done in 1954.[52] By 1960, twenty men

---

[50] If you are in the Albany, NY, area, I run what is basically this program for teens: www.BrianHuskie.com

[51] *How America's Leading Science Fiction Authors Are Shaping Your Future* by Eileen Gunn http://www.smithsonianmag.com/arts-culture/how-americas-leading-science-fiction-authors-are-shaping-your-future-180951169/

[52] *What We Mortals Can Learn From the 4-Minute Mile* by Matt Frazier http://www.nomeatathlete.com/4-minute-mile-certainty/

had broken the four-minute mile, and in 1964, a high school junior did it. Today, four minutes is the standard for professional middle-distance runners. This is the power of Youtube and other sites on the internet. I just finished watching a video where a teenager built a functioning submarine. Whatever anyone else has done, you can do. Does that seem pie-in-the-sky? Maybe, but someone else *did* do it, and weren't they human, like you? Don't they live in the same world as you? Then what are you waiting for?

Projects are completely self-directed, but may come under the guidance of adults, peers, and the community. Projects may take the form of internships or apprenticeships, or they may be individual or group endeavors with some specific goal, such as repair a junk car, take pictures from outer space, build an aquaponics system, start a business, write a novel, or learn calculus. This program requires one *major* project per trimester. You're limited only by your capacity and imagination, but here is a list of project suggestions:

1. Aquaponics: learn what it is, and build one of any size.
2. Ask ten strangers of all backgrounds to recommend one book. With help from others, collect these in one place and read them.[53]*
3. Build a weather balloon/camera apparatus to take pictures from outer space.
4. Attend someone else's place of worship. Make comparisons to your own.*
5. Analyze the components of friendship. Write three hundred words on the subject. Read your essay aloud into a tape recorder. Listen to yourself; figure out

---

[53] Every project with an asterisk comes from *We Need Experience More Than We Need Algebra* by John Taylor Gatto
http://www.lifelearningmagazine.com/1212/we-need-experience-more-than-we-need-algebra.htm

how to improve your performance. Do so.*

6. Apprentice yourself for one day to your mother. Do the same with your father. And for a neighbor or a stranger.*

7. At your supermarket, select twenty packaged food items at random. Calculate how many miles they traveled from point-of-origin to reach you.*

8. Bicycle fifty miles, at least, to a new place.*

9. Boat part of the Great Loop (or all of it!)

10. Build a canoe.

11. Build a drone or learn to fly model planes, submarines, etc.

12. Build a dwelling (cobb house, tiny house, doghouse, dollhouse, etc.).

13. Build an obstacle course.

14. Build something from the beginning – a wall, a box, a simple shelter.*

15. Buy a cup of coffee for a self-made millionaire (or some other definition of success) and have a professional conversation with them

16. Canoe part of the Northern Forest Canoe Trail (or all of it!)

17. Catch and clean/cook a fish. Eat it the same hour.*

18. Change the motor oil in the family car; also the fan belt and windshield wipers.*

19. Conduct an experiment.

20. Learn to apply cosmetics for a variety of people and events.

21. Create an app.

22. Create and showcase your greatest works of art, both somewhere terrestrial and cyber.

23. Design clothing for friends, family, or clients.

24. Do some research, then visit the five most prosperous businesses in your area; observe them externally for a day, then attempt to be given an internal tour. Take notes.*

25. Do something in front of a large audience (magic,

standup comedy, a Ted talk, etc.).

26. Follow the trash from your home, step by step, from its origin to its final resting place.*

27. Follow your electricity to its source.*

28. Get rejected, on purpose, every day for one hundred days (and keep a journal or a blog).

29. Give yourself one week to learn something seemingly impossible (calculus, Spanish, etc.) then teach it to someone else.

30. Go thirty days (or longer) without any electronics.

31. Grow enough vegetables for one meal. Cook and eat it.*

32. Have a conversation with a well-known (or famous) person

33. Hike the Forty-six Adirondack High Peaks (possibly in the winter), or set some other outdoor goal.

34. Hike part of the Appalachian Trail (or the whole thing!).

35. Hike the last hundred miles of the Appalachian Trail without resupply.

36. Host a dinner party to raise money for a cause (proper etiquette, cooking, budgeting, etc.)

37. Host or participate in a cooking contest (record it and post it on Youtube)

38. Stephen King wrote: *If you wrote something for which someone sent you a check, if you cashed the check and it didn't bounce, and if you then paid the light bill with the money, I consider you talented.* Write something and get paid for it.

39. Intern/volunteer/get a job (that's not fast food or box stores...e.g., shadow someone interesting at work).

40. Interview somebody over ninety-years-old about their life and opinions about topics of current interest. Ask them to discuss the greatest differences. Interview someone under seven in the same fashion *

41. Involve yourself in local government (push for a

change, support a candidate, conduct a letter-writing campaign, etc.).

42. Kill and clean a small animal. Cook and eat it.*
43. Landscape.
44. Learn about herbal medicine and apply what you've learned.
45. Learn handyman skills and use them (plumbing, electrical, drywall, etc.).
46. Learn how to whittle, build furniture, or other fine woodworking.
47. Learn outdoor survival skills.
48. Learn performance skills (e.g. juggling).
49. Learn to fly a plane (Wes Beach describes a teenager who did just that in his book *Self-Directed Learning: Documentation and Life Stories*).
50. Look at apartments as if you were a potential renter. Be safe, bring a friend.
51. Organize and manage a sports team or start a league of your own.
52. Participate in or organize a historical reenactment.
53. Pay your parents' bills (or maybe just their utilities) for a month.
54. Pick a daily newspaper. Read every single word. Underline as you read.*
55. Plant a little tree; care for it for three years; keep notes on its progress and setbacks.*
56. Produce/act/direct a play or movie.
57. Raise meat animals...or better yet, insects...for personal consumption.
58. Raise money for a cause
59. Read twenty-five (or fifty...or seventy-five...or one hundred) books.
60. Remain silent for a full day.*
61. Repair a junk car until it passes inspection.
62. Research/take lessons in method acting. Spend a day as a different sex.*
63. Select a book on a topic for which you have no

interest. Read it in a single sitting cover to cover.*

64. Sell home-made fudge on the street. Create advertising signs for your table.*

65. Sleep out-of-doors under the stars all by yourself for two consecutive nights.*

66. Spend a full day all by yourself in a wild place.*

67. Start a band, play in a band, or learn an instrument.

68. Start a small business.

69. Start an underground newsletter.

70. Start at least five conversations with complete strangers, and do more listening than speaking.

71. Struggle to repair a damaged relationship.*

72. Swim a lengthy distance (or in icy water).

73. Take and pass college credit bearing tests (e.g., CLEP). Do this at least once, even if you don't plan on going to college.

74. Take college classes (for credit or sit-in).

75. Throw away three (or five…or ten) things a day for ninety days and log them online.

76. Track your water supply to its source; diagram its route.*

77. Tutor or teach a particular subject.

78. Visit ten (or twenty…or thirty) historical sites, museums, aquariums, etc.

79. Visit the wholesale food markets for your city/region. Find out procedures to shop there as a customer. Do you need licenses? *

80. Volunteer abroad.

81. Volunteer to tutor reading or math in elementary school, first grade.*

82. Walk ten full miles to a place you never were.*

83. Walk, bike, or drive a significant distance (across New York, across New England, across the country, etc.).

84. Watch three TV shows for which you have no interest. Take notes.*

85. Work with the family budget, make your own budget, and plan your own retirement.

86. Write a book (at least 50,000 words). Take a page from NaNoWriMo and complete the book in a month.
87. Write advertisements or parody advertisements and upload them to Youtube.

Rhetoric (Writing and Speaking)

Our ability to speak and write, to persuade, to form relationships, and to articulate our thoughts and feelings, is the bedrock of success. Students have very little opportunity to exercise personal expression that is meaningful to them in school – they are too busy writing other people's essays to be graded based on other people's rubrics.

In my experience as a teacher, I have noticed that the one time students have an authentic opportunity for self-expression, it's their senior year when it's time to write their "common app" (college admissions essay). For most students, this is a struggle. For one, there is no rubric, so they don't know how to write it. For another, they are to write about something that was meaningful to them and that demonstrates personal growth through struggle, and they can't find anything to write about – they've spent too much time in safe, predictable, boring classrooms. This is why so many essays have something to do with sports or some other extracurricular activity.

Most scholarship committees look for similar essays, by the way. Typically they will look at the quality of writing and the significance of experience. In attempting to be proactive with my seniors, and looking for scholarships and working alongside them, I discovered that, for one, nothing too significant happened to them during high school, and second, they wouldn't know how to write about it if it did.

Each trimester students are to choose the most significant project they worked on and write a 650 to 2,000 word reflection. Students must also write a 650 to 2,000 word essay detailing some aspect of their volunteer work, and how they have grown from the experience as a person. Finally, the culminating experience will include a recorded interview and/or a presentation to a panel of experts, based on one of those essays.

Graduation Requirements

In order to be considered for graduation, students must:

- Complete and document 500 hours of volunteer service.
- Complete a minimum of one major project; complete one major project per semester (the number of projects completed will depend on when you plan to "graduate").
- Between projects and volunteer service, be able to defend that coursework or experience was had in each of the following subjects:
  o English (literature)
  o Social Studies (history)
  o Math
  o Science
  o Health
  o Physical education
  o Art & music
- All writing in the "Writing and Speaking" component must be complete, plus a 1,500 – 3,000 word "exit" essay, arguing why you have earned a high school diploma, what your strengths are, how you are ready for adult life despite not having the typical high school experience, and what your next steps will be.
- Obtain three letters of recommendation, only one of which may be from an immediate relative.

15

POST HIGH SCHOOL:
A MESSAGE FOR SCHOOL
BOARDS AND SCHOOL
ADMINISTRATORS

How might a school board, in cooperation with school administrators, structure a school to remain compliant with state mandates as well as union contracts, while at the same time respecting students enough to entrust them with the freedom to control their education? Carl Rogers wrote a book back in 1969 titled *Freedom to Learn*. In chapter two, *A College Professor Gives Freedom Within Limits*, he shares Dr. Faw's methods for approaching his introductory class *Fundamentals of Psychology*. Dr. Faw's stated goals are to offer opportunities for creativity and a wide variety of student productions, without jettisoning rigorous academic standards. Faw was also concerned with teachers relying on *elicited* responses as opposed to *emitted* responses from students. An *elicited* response is that thing that teachers do when they have a specific answer in their head, and they call on students until someone says that one thing the teacher is thinking of. I admit that I'm guilty, too, and it's mostly a useless exercise. The focus is on the teacher, who demands a response from their stimuli, much as a scientist might attempt to elicit a response from an animal by making a loud noise.

An *emitted* response gives priority to the subject – you present a problem to the animal and watch them attempt to work out a solution, without additional instruction or coaching. Dr. Peter Gray, author of *Free to Learn*, writes on his blog about an experiment that resulted in thousands of impoverished kids becoming computer literate within three months.[54] All that was done was a computer was installed into the outside wall of a building in a New Delhi slum. No instruction was given. Hundreds of kids, through play, learned how to:

> *Use all Windows operational functions, such as click, drag, open, close, resize, minimize, menus, navigation, etc.; Draw and paint with the computer; Load and save files; Play games; Run educational and other programs; Browse and surf the Internet; Set up email accounts; Send and receive email; Chat on the Internet; Do simple troubleshooting, for example, if the speakers are not working; Download and play streaming media; Download games.*

This experiment was repeated a number of times in a variety of places, with similar results. Think about it. If I were to show you how to open a puzzle box, you'd have far less fun with it, and learn less, than if you figured it out yourself. I believe this is what the poem "Introduction to Poetry" by Billy Collins is all about: *I say drop a mouse into a poem/ and watch him probe his way out...But all they want to do/ is tie the poem to a*

---

[54] *Minimally Invasive Education: Lessons from India*
https://www.psychologytoday.com/blog/freedom-learn/200901/minimally-invasive-education-lessons-india

chair with rope/ and torture a confession out of it.

In Carl Rogers' book, Professor Faw separated these two groups into the *Respondent Group* (you respond to what the teacher directs you to do, or, as Collins would say, you have a confession tortured out of you) and the *Operant Group* (operate on the subject matter as a mouse works his way out of a maze):

Number and type of productions in operant and respondent groups

	Respondent Group N 38	Operant Group N 38
Statement of goals	0	26
Journal articles reported	0	165
Research proposals	0	25
Experiments (original)	0	18
Group projects	0	3
Demonstrations	0	2
Library studies (term papers)	38	8
Field trips	0	23
Vocational test batteries	5	7
Counseling	0	1
HDI program	0	19
Interview with instructor	0	32
Other activities	0	4
Course examinations	190	190
Total productions	233	523
Mean number	6.1	13.7

Simply looking at the data, it's obvious that the breadth of experiences had by students was far greater in the group given freedom. Each student also produced more than twice as much in the operant group than in the respondent group. There is nothing to indicate that there was less rigor just because there was more freedom – you may infer, based on the very brief descriptions of the *productions*, that the students with the benefit of freedom had a *more* rigorous experience. Certainly their experiences resonated with them more than a term paper and a couple of tests could.

In course evaluations, some students in the operant group said this:

- "This has been the most exciting course I have ever taken."
- "The whole experience was extremely rewarding and I must admit that the procedures followed in the teaching of this course was first rate."
- "It is a good course for most students but is less appealing to the fairly rigid type student who wants direction or who wants to please the teacher."
- "The course emphasizes the importance of the active learner as opposed to the passive learner."
- "The course placed a premium on creativity rather than mere memorization, on planning instead of conforming to the plans of other, on problem solving rather than recall."
- "The course recognized individual differences and permitted a great variety in types of productivity."
- "The teacher's role in the class was different than in a traditional class. He didn't seem to play the part of an authority but tried to stimulate students to discover things for himself. He occupied the center of the stage less than the usual course."

- "The course motivated students more than the average course and more closely met the needs of most students."

Generally speaking, if there was a board of education or some other governing entity sympathetic to this style of education, here's how I would suggest they structure the school to respect and trust students, while hopefully remaining in compliance with various contracts and edicts (at least in a secondary school). I would assign students to a teacher. If average class size is twenty-five students, that would be twenty-five students per teacher. Hopefully it is less than that, it could be more, but a certain number of students would be assigned to a teacher, and that teacher would become advisor to those students:

- Teachers design learning experiences that are approximately fifteen school days long. Those learning experiences are aligned with their certifications (though teachers are free to co-offer and cross-list courses), and published in a catalog the quarter or semester prior. There should be some opportunity for students to suggest learning opportunities.
- The catalog of learning experiences should contain all pertinent information, such as which teacher(s) is offering it and their contact information, how many credits the experience is worth, in which disciplines, how many students are able to register, whether or not there's a "part two," and, of course, a succinct and accurate description of the experience (much of the mechanics may be under guidance of school administration). All of this information must also be made available to parents.
- Grades are not necessary. Students fulfill the requirements of the experience and receive credit, or

they don't. Students should complete an anonymous course evaluation at the end that is submitted to the school administrator and reviewed by the instructor, and that is taken seriously when considering offering the course again, or what topics are included in the course, or the method by which the course was taught.

- There is time built into the schedule for two "classes" a day, i.e., the fifteen day learning experiences. In a one-hundred-eighty day school year, that's twenty-four opportunities for learning experiences per year.
  - o To use New York state credit requirements as an example, students are *required* to earn a minimum of 22 credits in specific disciplines (1 credit is usually 1 year-long course). Two of those credits are in physical education, which could be reasonably covered in the first and/or last periods of the day. Therefore, students need 5 additional credits per year to be on track to graduate within four years. Each learning experience, depending on what it entails, could be worth anything from ¼ to ½ credit in one or more disciplines.
  - o Two hours a day, multiplied by fifteen days, is thirty hours. That's approximately how much time a student spends in a classroom for one quarter of an academic school year. Of course, if the learning experience is project based or if options for additional "productions" (such as Dr. Faw's model), and the student is required to do much more than sit around in a classroom all day, you could probably argue for ½ of a credit.
- Experiences could be offered over the summer, as well.
- Learning experiences need not be project based or

experiential – although I believe those methods are generally superior to, say, traditional lectures, there are certainly some students who would love an advanced lecture-style course on calculus. We miss the point if this entire model seeks to just have school exactly as it is, but with a different schedule. The point is an academic environment that is student-centered, where there is enough option and freedom to foster curiosity and creativity. I don't mean to be dogmatic, or to be dogmatic about not being dogmatic. Keep in mind the mouse figuring its way out of the maze – that may include some lecture courses, as well as Dr. Faw's model, as well as project-based, as well as work-study (internships/volunteer work), etc.

- There should be plenty of opportunities for learning experiences both on and off campus.
- Students have a list of requirements necessary for graduation. There is an advisory period that exists to assist students in tracking their own progress and to sign up for appropriate learning blocks, to help them through any personal or academic issues they are having in school, and to assist with post-high school planning.
- A suggested schedule:
  - 8:00am – 9:00am: students check in with their advisor and let the advisor know where they are going. This is the advisory/physical activity period. In the scenario that there are twenty-five students, twenty of them will run off to the basketball courts, track, weight room, etc., to start their day off with physical movement. Five of them will stay behind with their advisor.
  - 9:00am – 11:00am: Learning Experience One.
  - 11:00am – 12:00am: Lunch & study period.

o 12:00am – 2:00pm: Learning Experience Two.
o 2:00pm – 3:00pm: Optional advisory period, study period, open gym, guidance counselor meetings, course registrations, etc.

A sample transcript might look something like this:

**Excelsior Central
High School**

Suzy Student	**Freshman Year Transcript**	
Class	**Discipline**	**Credits**
VA Hospital, volunteer	Health	0.25
Aquaponics, design and build	Science	0.25
Community religions and place of worship field experiences	Social Studies	0.25
Journalism	English	0.25
Personal finance	Math	0.25
15 days of rejection (plus blog)	English	0.25
Historical Reenactment, Battle of the Bulge	Social Studies	0.25
Historical Reenactment, Famous American Speeches	Social Studies	0.25
Gardening and food preparation	Science	0.25
Intro to Robotics	Math	0.25
Novel Writing	English	0.25

Public Speaking	English	0.25
Nursing Home, volunteer	Social Studies	0.25
Elementary School, tutor	English	0.25
Local government, volunteer	Social Studies	0.25
Intro to Algebra	Math	0.25
Sculpting	Art	0.25
Song writing	Music	0.25
Ordering food in a Spanish Restaurant	Foreign Language	0.25
Exercising your constitutional rights	Social Studies	0.25
Algebra Regents Exam Prep	Math	0.25
Living Environments Regents Exam Prep	Science	0.25
How to earn college scholarships	Elective	0.25
Basic car maintenance	Elective	0.25
Daily	Phys Ed	1.00
	Total Credits:	7.00

Requirements (NY)	Credits Required for Graduation	Credits earned Freshman Year	% Complete
English	4	1.25	31%
Social Studies	4	1.5	38%
Science	3	0.75	25%

Math	3	1	33%
Foreign Language	1	0.25	25%
Art, Music, Dance, Theater	1	0.5	50%
Physical Education	2	1	50%
Health	0.5	0.25	50%
Electives	3.5	0.5	14%
Totals	**22**	**7**	**32%**

This is not a description of what I think would be a "perfect" school. This is a description of what I believe to be a very good school, that could be compliant with state mandates and with union contracts, and that is student-centered within the milieu of compulsory education.[55] Two hour "learning experiences" that happen twice a day for fifteen days gives students approximately the same amount of per-class "seat time" as an academic quarter, but allows students to focus on just two things at a time, rather than bounce around between many different unrelated subjects for a very brief period of time, every day for 180 or 190 days. It takes away some of the psychic violence of compulsion by taking away grades, and focuses on the experiences themselves. It offers students invitations to sign up for classes, giving some semblance of mutual consent, and does not take very seriously the student's academic grade level (freshman through seniors could all reasonably sign up for any one of the classes listed in the sample transcript above). Students have multiple opportunities to rate, anonymously or in person, the effectiveness and relevance of a class, and to suggest classes in the future, and to have those suggestions accommodated.

---

[55] I would also suggest schools that have absolutely no more than 250 people, students and employees included, as per Dunbar, although I admit that this is often beyond our control; https://en.wikipedia.org/wiki/Dunbar%27s_number

CONCLUSION

More and more people are waking up to the truth that standardized assessments, school funding, state standards, federal involvement in education, billionaires and their charter schools, or any other flavor-of-the-day-Diane-Ravitch-style-edu-controversy, are all mostly symptoms (or sometimes pure distractions), and that the problem is compulsion – even more to the root, the problem is the threat of violence implied by compulsion. You cannot bring peace and love with compulsion that is backed up by violence any more than you can bring freedom through military occupation, and the more powerful and omnipresent compulsory school is in your family's life, the more the threat of violence looms over you.

It would satisfy my ego immensely to sell a million copies of this book, but if a million copies sell, and nothing changes, then I'm afraid that we've all wasted our time. Do me a favor. If you are in middle or high school, or you know someone who is, have them honestly grade themselves on this rubric. If you score all "zeros" and "ones", then you're my kind of person! You're also trapped. Read this book and others like it; seek out like-minded people; most of all, take control of your life and your future. It's not anyone else's but yours.

Thank you for reading, and I invite you to connect with me at www.BrianHuskie.com.

	0	**1**	**2**
Goals: *how much do you care about what it is I told you that you're supposed to be able to know or do?*	I was warned. I was given an explanation. Nevertheless, I persisted in believing that your goals for me are not my goals for myself.	I have entered into a Cold-War style agreement of *mutually assured destruction.* I will set just enough goals to ensure that you can do a reasonably good job, in hopes that I am not bothered too often.	Your goals are my goals. You want me to do chapter summaries? Done. Pythagorean theorem? You bet. Golden Age of Greece? More like Golden Age of self-selecting my own goals from your prescribed list of approved goals! I am very excited to blindly trust authority with the direction of my life.

| *Self-regulation:* *how seriously do you take the process of meeting the goals I've told you to set for yourself?* | I have made the decision to not take the advice that I hadn't asked for, and therefore will live my life incapable of basic twenty-first century skills, such as making inferences and working with others. | Instead of choosing to be a dead salmon in the middle of a fast-moving river, going with the flow, I've chosen to be a dead salmon on the river bank, just lying and rotting. | I carefully and painstakingly reach my goals based on the apt, cogent, and timely feedback that you give me, and I am surprised yet gratified to see how nicely the result resembles everybody else's results. |

Your Grades: *How important is it to you what a series of strangers think about your capacity to know or do; how seriously do you take their quantification of your academic worth, down to a single percentage point?*	I have chosen to not take my grades seriously, and therefore there is no way to hold me accountable. I will continue to make my own decisions for my own life until I am forced into an alternative placement or am rejected by the system entirely.	I have internalized years of mediocre grades and now believe I am a mediocre person. I am willing to do just enough to pass, but I view it as an economic transaction rather than an opportunity for self-betterment, e.g., doing these things gets me enough points to be released from this place.	I know that the numeric valuation of the one thing that separates me from an animal – my capacity for abstract thought – is valid and reliable. How you rate me is very important and I've learned to do just about anything in exchange for this extrinsic reward. I also appreciate your affirmation of my superiority over my peers.

*Students who do not write in blue or black ink or request written permission to use the bathroom, who socialize with peers in class, or who skip class to go waste time in the world, may score no more than a "1" in all categories.

BRIAN HUSKIE

ABOUT BRIAN

Brian Huskie is the founder and director of *Huskie's Heroes*. He is a National Board Certified High School English teacher with more than ten years of experience and a degree in School Administration, founder of the Albany High/Capital District Refugee Scholarship Endowment, an Operation Iraqi Freedom veteran, and author of *A White Rose: A Soldier's Story of Love, War, and School*. Brian and his wife, Ramita, homeschool their two boys in Albany, NY.

Connect with Brian at www.BrianHuskie.com and https://www.facebook.com/BrianHuskieAuthor/

Made in the USA
Columbia, SC
12 January 2018